The New
Tax Guide for
Performers, Writers,
Directors, Designers,
and other
Show Biz Folk

The New Tax Guide for Performers, Writers, Directors, Designers, and other Show Biz Folk

Fifth Edition
Revised and Updated

R. Brendan Hanlon

LIMELIGHT EDITIONS

New York

Fifth Limelight Edition January 1999
Fourth Limelight Edition January 1996
Third Limelight Edition January 1994
Revised and Updated Edition January 1991
First Limelight Edition December 1988

Printed and bound in Canada by Webcom

Library of Congress Cataloging-in-Publication Data

Hanlon, R. Brendan, 1936–
The new tax guide for performers, writers, directors, designers, and other show biz folk / R. Brendan Hanlon.—Rev. and updated.
    p.   cm.
ISBN 0-87910-148-2
1. Entertainers—Taxation—Law and legislation—United States.
2. Theatrical producers and directors—Taxation—Law and legislation—United States. 3. Set designers—Taxation—Law and
legislation—United States. I. Title. KF6369.8.E57H37 1991
343.7305'2'024791—dc20
[347.30352024791]   90–40432
                                            CIP

For Marjorie and Nell, astortha, for Eren Ozker who gave great

presents, and for Creighton Barrow who wrote . . .

What Would Have Happened Had He Showed?

A work by a playwright named Becket
(*Godot*) was oft' thought to be dreck, yet,
Without using seduction
In every production
They manage to get an erect set.

Contents

Foreword
Return Engagements

Since I've been in the income tax "dodge" (an apt phrase), I have seen many tax laws come and go. Political pressure, the need to control the economy, and special interest needs govern the passage of tax law. Some of the tax laws are memorable to me because favorite deductions were eliminated (e.g., office in the home—Tax Reform Act of 1976) or they merely had catchy names (TEFRA—Tax Equity and Fiscal Responsibility Act). Isn't it just like the government to employ acronyms? I wonder what pea-brain first figured out how to pronounce TEFRA? Well, I have jumped on the bandwagon with the other pea-brains. I have my own acronym, which you'll discover if you read this book. But it can't be pronounced!

Over the years I've had this sinking feeling that things were only getting worse. When the reports of the Tax Reform Act of 1986 started appearing in the tax press, horror filled the hearts of the tax observers of the land, mine among them. The Senate version of tax reform wasn't much different from that "joke" Form 1040, which has been circulating for some time in various graphic forms: (1) How much did you make last year? and (2) Send it in! The Senate wanted to lower tax rates and do away with just about every deduction you could think of. The House version wasn't nearly so unrealistic as far as professionals and the middle class were concerned: It kept business deductions but put them all on Schedule A and introduced the detested 2 percent floor. This latter version was the one that prevailed and survived the joint committee and became the law. It was in committee that the provision for "certain performing artists with an adjusted gross income (AGI) under $16,000, with two or more employers . . ." was born. My personal feeling is that this provision was "crumbs from the nobility's table." The best I can say about it is that it's better than nothing. Increased standard deductions and exemptions are supposed to make up for the loss of the 2 percent of AGI. That's all well and good for the average worker who has few, if any, deductions, but Congress has either never heard of, or doesn't give a damn for, a whole class of workers: the freelance professional who as often as not is paid a salary and therefore is not qualified to use Schedule C to file. Or the variation on the theme: The professional who is paid sometimes on the books and sometimes off the books for doing *the same damn thing!*

The Constitution is supposed to assure all citizens equal treatment under the law, but I'll be fried if I can see how the Internal Revenue Code—any version you want to select from the '30s on—can give equal treatment when it refuses to recognize that there are very complex situations in the economic life of some taxpayers. As long as these reforming politicians stick to their simpleminded notion that the Tax Code should be simple and that fairness will follow, certain classes of taxpayers are simply going to continue to get the long, green weenie. Life isn't simple and tax law shouldn't be. Until the law recognizes the special circumstances of performing artists and other salaried freelancers, there will be no equal treatment for them. The 100,000-odd performing artists and other "support personnel" will get that equal treatment only when special interest legislation is passed allowing *all* established freelance professionals to use Schedule C. And, incidentally, that would mean that New York City would have to exempt them from the evil Unincorporated Business Tax.

If you, dear Reader, are one of those freelance professionals and you'd like to stop getting the weenie, start writing letters! Get informed and start writing!

To get you informed, I couldn't recommend a better book for openers than *Louis Rukeyser's Business Almanac*. Read chapter eleven. Then, check the index for references to the Tax Reform Act. This whole first phase of your tax education will take about ten minutes. Can you spare it? Your eyes will be opened. A few goodies therefrom:

In 1987 the American Taxpayer spent in the neighborhood of 1.7 billion hours filling in tax forms. Of that, 105 million hours were added by the tax "reform" act of 1986. Between 1967 and 1987:

• receipts from personal income taxes grew 532%.
• receipts from social insurance taxes grew 898%.
• receipts from total federal taxes grew 504%.
• consumer prices grew 240%.

Total tax receipts for all governments—federal, state, and city—averages out to $4,954 per American, for '86.

The Tax Foundation in Washington tells us that you had to work until May 4 for the government. After that you could start to keep some of your own money!

In 1984 there were fourteen tax brackets for a couple married and filing jointly. They ranged from 11% ($3,400 to $5,500) to 50% of everything over $162,400. Starting in 1988, there are two tax brackets, 1 5% and 28%. A married couple need have a net taxable income of only $29,700 or more to be in the same tax bracket as Donald Trump and the little woman!

For years, the Supreme Court has been struggling to define obscenity; I just did it for 'em!

As I live in Massachusetts, I write to Senator Kerry and my congressman, Gerry Studds. They give great response. In 1986, they were very helpful and did what they could to present the plight of performers to the "Packwoods" who were in the process of perpetrating the Tax Reform Act of 1986. Have *you* ever written to your senators and representatives? It works! They tell us one letter carries the weight of ten telephone calls.

Another thing you must do is support your union's efforts to get beneficial legislation, and if your union is making no effort to get beneficial legislation, then badger your union to make efforts . . . to get . . . beneficial . . . legislation. Equity has recently formed a Legislative Committee. Make your feelings known to the committee. Ask that *Equity News* and other union organs report what's happening in Congress that affects you and encourage the membership to write to Congress. *You* are your unions. How can you get so passionate about Waiver Theatres and ignore it when Congress waivers your goddam deductions right out the window so that tax legislation can remain "revenue neutral" and those bandits can make speeches saying they didn't raise taxes. Of course they didn't raise taxes. They just *raised* everyone's NET TAXABLE INCOME! Have you seen the statistics in the *Business Almanac?*

I want you to know that by doing a little in '86, we got a better-than-nothing provision that provides a measure of relief to a few performers. Think what could happen if we did a lot! Get off your duff and do something!

Also while you're at it, tell your friends to buy this book, not any other ones, just buy this one. Now shut up and let me get rich in piece (*sic*)!

Plum Nearly
Marshfield, Massachusetts

As of the summer of '95, a *flat tax* is a real possibility. I cannot think of a worse disaster for free-lance professionals who are predominantly on salary. If flat tax legislation ever makes it to the Senate or House, you'd better organize and get active, *"and, by opposing, end a sea of troubles".* The only way you all would be saved is if Congress passed legislation making performing artists and performing arts support personnel *Statutory Employees.* This would allow you to file with the same tax benefits as insurance sales persons by using Schedule C, q. v. Why don't you start working on it now? If you don't know what I'm talking about, get a copy of this book and read it. The topic comes up in several places. Never mind where. It'll do you good to hunt for it.

Yours truly,
Roundleigh Beaton

Introduction

If you think baseball is the national pastime, you're mistaken. It's avoiding taxes, reducing taxes, getting out of taxes, or, at least, postponing taxes. And it's not a simple matter. A book making "taxes" simple is an impossibility. I can't make taxes simple, but I can make them less hard. This is not a "do-it-yourself" manual enabling you to prepare your own tax return. If your return is at all complicated, it is well worth the cost of having it prepared by a competent tax person who knows the performing arts (hereinafter referred to as "the Biz").

I am attempting to correct a lot of misinformation circulated backstage, dispel a lot of myths, but mainly to formulate guidelines for *good record keeping* with an eye to accomplishing two goals:

1. You should get your "just desserts" when your return is prepared for you: the lowest legal tax (or the biggest refund, however you care to look at it). Justice Louis D. Brandeis said that it is the moral duty of every taxpayer to pay the smallest tax!
2. Should your return be selected for audit examination, you can make a comprehensive accounting of your income and expenses and not pay any additional tax.

It is implicit in the expression "record keeping" that someone keep records. Tax law requires that someone keep your records and that someone is *you!*

Record keeping needn't be a lot of work. It's largely a matter of developing some habits.

Taxation is based on laws made by congressmen, with all the attendant argument, litigation, and interpretation one might expect to result from the efforts of that group. One is, therefore, tempted to leave no stone unturned in bringing the gospel to novitiates, to cover every possibility, to pen the absolute and final authoritative source of tax information for show folk. I'm not qualified to do that; no one is. The result would be a self-defeating quagmire of technical language and you might as well reproduce the Internal Revenue Code instead. A certain amount of technicality is necessary to reduce misinterpretation, but I have written this book much in the way I talk to my own clients, in the vernacular.

As far as taxes are concerned, there is really little difference between performers and their backstage brethren. Performers have some dozen or so more deductions. There is, however, a different *treatment* of deductions and the income of *salaried employees* and *self-employed* persons. I have attempted to flag these differences along the way, so all you full-time and part-time self-employed writers, designers, directors, choreographers, and so forth, keep a weather-eye peeled!

Our politicians are forever "reforming" the tax laws, so this tome will be current only as of the last printing of this edition. Deductions come and deductions go, so CWYTP! (Check with your tax preparer!)

A word of advice on how to use this book. By all means, read through it once. More, if you're so inclined. But don't expect to file all the information away in your brain. You want to develop the "habits" I referred to above—habits of record keeping—but the details of what to keep track of are too many to retain. So use the book as a reference source, a traveling companion, a travel diary, and you may find preparing your taxes a lot easier.

The New
Tax Guide for
Performers, Writers,
Directors, Designers,
and other
Show Biz Folk

1

Money
Some Questions and Answers

You get it and you spend it. It comes in and it goes out. Most of it is taxable, some of it isn't. Some of it is earned by you, some of it earns its own income. You exchange it for consumer goods, put it to work, throw it away, give it away: It lets you live. If you earn, or your money earns, enough in any given year, the law of the land says you must account for it and, maybe, pay tax on it.

What is nontaxable money?

Here are some examples of nontaxable money:

- Federal tax refunds
- Certain gifts
- Accident, health, casualty, and life insurance proceeds
- Bequests and inheritances
- Child support
- V.A. disability payments

These sources are not taxable federally, but may or may not require reporting on your state or local tax form. CWYTP. If you are uncertain about the taxability of any money you receive, check with the folks who gave it to you. They should know, although they are not always correct and frequently are noncommittal.

Should you keep a record of nontaxable money?

Mais, oui, mes amis! Si, si, si; da, da, da! . . . YES! FER SURE!

Why?

You may get audited by the IRS and have to identify deposited amounts in your checking and savings accounts. If you can't demonstrate that the money is nontaxable, the IRS will assume it is taxable and tax it!

If you had a poor year and get audited, you will want to be able to answer the inevitable questions from the examiner: "How did you live?" If you can't show nontaxable sources, sufficient deductions might be disallowed to bring your taxable income up to a certain standard of living and your tax will be recalculated. In short, you will *owe!*

How can you keep a record of nontaxable money?

Don't rely on memory! Make notes! Note gifts of money in your diary and indicate the source. Annotate all your deposit slips:

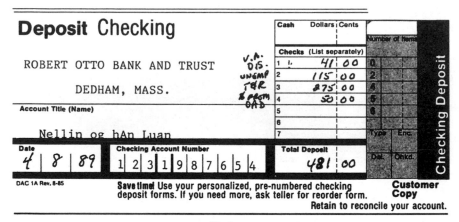

Fig. 1

In Figure 1, $91 is nontaxable: the Veteran's Disability and the birthday money from Dad. Even if an IRS auditor didn't accept this, it would serve to remind you of the source and you could obtain verification that would do the trick.

What are some examples of taxable money?

1. *Earned*—money given you in exchange for goods or services: salaries, tips, wages, commissions, royalties, fees, and the fair market value of "barter" income (whether in the form of exchanged services or goods).
2. *Nonearned*—money that your money earns: bank interest, dividends on investments, income or (loss) from partnerships, trusts, estates, farms, alimony, gambling, prizes, lotteries, quiz shows, rental property, royalties (not the authors' kind), sale or exchange of capital assets or property, unemployment compensation, and so forth.

If you earn money, are you an employee or a self-employed person?

Either! The distinction is made in the Social Security laws. Roughly speaking, an employee is someone who performs services for another person or company in exchange for payment of money or goods or services that have a determinable value. An employee performs those services under that other person's control, on his or her premises, at times and with the regularity determined by that person. Usually remuneration is set at an hourly, weekly, or annual basis. That other person or company has control over *how* one performs the services, *when* one performs the services, *if* one completes the services, and the *result* of the services. If the employer's control is limited to the *result only,* one is probably self-employed, an independent contractor, a freelancer. In performing arts contexts, people who operate as freelancers are often paid a salary, and tax treatment becomes a gray area and distinctions blur. There are some tax advantages (dealt with later) to filing as a self-employed person. (The Republic of Ireland has the most civilized scheme of all: An established artist pays no tax at all on money earned from artistic endeavors! *Erin go bragh!*)

What are some of the apparent differences between an employee and a self-employed person?

An employee gets a salary or wages; a freelancer gets fees or commissions or royalties. An employee has taxes withheld from his pay; a self-employed person does not and, therefore, must pay estimated taxes (see page 12). An employee can collect unemployment compensation; not so a freelancer. An employee is covered by Workmen's Compensation Insurance; a freelancer is not. An employee's Social Security contribution is matched by the employer; the self-employed person must pay self-employment tax all by himself.

Is it possible to be both an employee and a self-employed person?

Yes. You can, for example, teach design for a salary at a college and do shows for fees as an independent contractor; you can act on a soap opera for a salary and teach privately for fees. A performer might model or record books for fees and do union work for salary and be both fish and fowl and wind up in the soup.

Is it possible to be an employee but file as a self-employed person?

There has been, in recent years, frequent use by salaried performers of Schedule C—Profit or (Loss) from Business or Profession to report income and write off expenses. Their authority for using Schedule C is: *People have been getting away with it!*

There is no statute or case law, no rule or regulation, that allows this. So the answer to the question is "Not really." It would indeed be a lovely turn of events if the use of Schedule C by performers became authorized by law. Written any letters to Congress lately?

What records of income must an employee keep?

The worksheet portion of each W-4 form you fill out at the start of each job; an accurate daily record of tips declared and *not* declared to your employer; W-2 forms; Form 1099-MISC for miscellaneous compensation.

What other records of income should an employee keep?

Make diary annotations of salary and per diem payments. Keep check "stubs" or pay envelopes to verify W-2 forms and 1099-MISC. Keep copies of all your old tax returns.

When do you get your W-2 forms?

Sometimes when the job ends. But you're supposed to get one no later than January 31. If you don't get yours, you can't do your return, so inform your employer as soon as possible if the form is delayed. The W-2 form *must* be attached to the return.

I can't recommend strongly enough keeping a list of jobs as the year goes by (see Appendix I). Enter the producer's name, the name of the production, the name of the payroll company, if one has been used (they may be the ones responsible for the W-2 form), the number of exemptions you put down, and the date of the check as well as the date you receive it. You may get a check and then a W-2 from Cinema-Pay for a film you did for Spelvin Productions. Get it? So in the middle of February, when your tax appointment is imminent and you should have thirteen W-2 forms but you have only twelve, check your list to see who is missing.

It is not uncommon to receive money through SAG (Screen Actors Guild) for films or TV shows done years earlier. When one moves, usually one informs the unions but not some film company worked for several years earlier. The producers send the check to SAG and SAG, which has the correct address for you, sends it to you. The following February: no W-2, but you file anyway, and eleven months later you get a dread CP-2000 demanding tax, penalty, and interest. This can be avoided if you get your W-2 form. But why would you seek a W-2 form if you didn't know you were supposed to have one? So . . . if you get a residual or any other kind of payment and you have moved since the previous time you got a payment from the same source, inform the producer of your current address toot sweet! At year's end, as the W-2 forms roll in, check 'em off on the list to see if any are missing. If there are, make some calls. By law the producers must send the W-2 to you not to SAG, so save your breath and wonder not why SAG doesn't send you a W-2. It's not their job. It's your job to get address changes to the entire world.

What do they look like?

I wish I knew! There are many graphic variations on the theme, but they all have the same information on them. If you have earnings from more than one taxing jurisdiction paid by the same paymaster company, they may send more than one W-2 (duplicating or perhaps not duplicating the Federal information) and reporting earnings and withholding for a second or third state, etc.

What information is on a W-2 form?

Less than you think, for openers. The name of the producer may not be on it. The name of the production will probably NOT be on it. Here's what should be on it:

1. The calendar year, but *not* the specific dates you worked.
2. Your gross salary before withholding.
3. Withheld federal, state, and local income taxes.
4. Social security tax and medicare tax (FICA).
5. The amount on which your FICA is based (not always the same amount as gross wages).
6. Declared tips.
7. Other compensation (wardrobe allowances and so on).
8. Certain pension information.
9. State disability insurance.
10. If you receive a per diem instead of exact reimbursement from your employer and if the amount of the per diem exceeds what the government pays its employees in the same location, the *excess amount* will be included as compensation in box 10. The equivalent amount the government would have provided for that locality for the same period will be reported in box 17 after the code letter "L." If in certain locations you get more per diem than a government employee gets, you will have to account for it or pay tax on it.

Would you like to see some sample W-2 forms filled in and with their stories told in a fashion guaranteed to thrill even you?

Sure you would!

These samples happen to be 1992 W-2 forms. Although the graphics may change from one year to the next, the information is basically the same.

So, when you get your W-2 forms, pay attention to the headings of the boxes, not the box numbers. Campbell's may change its labels but the soup remains the same, and you may quote me.

Figure 2 is your common garden-variety W-2. You worked out of

1 Control number			OMB No. 1545-0008								
2 Employer's name, address, and ZIP code				6 Statutory employee ☐	Deceased ☐	Pension plan ☐	Legal rep ☐	942 emp. ☐	Subtotal ☐	Deferred compensation ☐	Void ☐

Sushie Dinner Theatre

Box 55, R.D. 4

Wasted, PA 19999

7 Allocated tips	8 Advance EIC payment
9 Federal income tax withheld 779.00	10 Wages, tips, other compensation 4905.00

3 Employer's identification number 22-1414114	4 Employer's state I.D. number 8560223	11 Social security tax withheld 507.78	12 Social security wages 4905.00
5 Employee's social security number		13 Social security tips	14 Medicare wages and tips

19 Employee's name, address, and ZIP code	15 Medicare tax withheld 118.76	16 Nonqualified plans

Ima Starr

945 West 55th St.

New York City,   10019

	17 See Instrs. for Box 17	18 Other

20	21	22 Dependent care benefits	23 Benefits included in Box 10

24 State income tax 81.90	25 State wages, tips, etc. 4905.00	26 Name of state PA	27 Local income tax 168.96	28 Local wages, tips, etc. 4905.00	29 Name of locality Phila

Copy B To Be Filed With Employee's FEDERAL Tax Return   Department of the Treasury—Internal Revenue Service

Form **W-2 Wage and Tax Statement 1992** (Rev. 4-92)

This information is being furnished to the Internal Revenue Service.

Fig. 2

town at a dinner theatre. You are a New York resident, but the Sushi Dinner Theatre is a Pennsylvania employer and pays that state's taxes. The employer paid you salary only. If he did pay for living expenses, it doesn't show on the W-2. If he provided room and/or board, it doesn't show on the W2. You would have to refer to a rider in your contract for this information.

The employer withheld Federal Income Tax (box 9), Pennsylvania State Income Tax (box 24), and Philadelphia City Tax (box 27).

Boxes 11 and 15 show 12.4 and 2.9 percent of your gross, respectively, withheld and matched by your employer to pay into your old age and medicare benefits, respectively. It totals 7.65%* of your gross no matter how many withholding exemptions you claim.

This W-2 does not reveal any other payroll deductions, such as state disability insurance, union dues collected, United Fund. Nor does it reveal when during the year you worked, how long you worked, or your weekly

*In these samples the 1992 rate is used.

gross. It shows only the gross amount earned, and the taxes withheld, as well as the fact that you are participating in a pension plan and ineligible, maybe, for an IRA.

Most of the W-2 forms you receive will be like this one (Figure 3). So, save your pay stubs and pay envelopes, which usually do have all the payroll deductions listed, show what period the payment covers, and indicate per diem, the rent on the cabin they've stuck you in, and so forth.

1 Control number			OMB No. 1545-0008								
2 Employer's name, address, and ZIP code Hamlet National Co. L.P. 2248 West 48th St. C/O Wink, Spinnaker & Boitano NY, NY 10069				6 Statutory employee ☐	Deceased ☐	Pension plan ☑	Legal rep. ☐	942 emp. ☐	Subtotal ☐	Deferred compensation ☐	Void ☐
				7 Allocated tips				8 Advance EIC payment			
				9 Federal income tax withheld 483.88				10 Wages, tips, other compensation 4014.74			
3 Employer's identification number 13-5555555555555		4 Employer's state I.D. number 876408		11 Social security tax withheld 242.40				12 Social security wages 3909.74			
5 Employee's social security number 123-45-6789				13 Social security tips				14 Medicare wages and tips 3909.74			
19 Employee's name, address, and ZIP code Bobby Otto 63 Avery St. Dedham, MA				15 Medicare tax withheld 56.69				16 Nonqualified plans			
				17 See Instrs. for Box 17 L 1185.00				18 Other			
20		21		22 Dependent care benefits				23 Benefits included in Box 10			
24 State income tax 166.18	25 State wages, tips, etc. 4014.74	26 Name of state NY		27 Local income tax 63.37		28 Local wages, tips. etc. 4014.74		29 Name of locality NYC			

Copy B To Be Filed With Employee's FEDERAL Tax Return   Department of the Treasury—Internal Revenue Service

Form **W-2 Wage and Tax Statement 1992** (Rev. 4-92)

This information is being furnished to the Internal Revenue Service.

Fig. 3

Now, in the next example, you're Bobby Otto, rising young star, on the road. You're in a tour of *Hamlet* by Jerome Francis X. O'Shaughnessy (born in Cork in 1570). Since the producer of this revival is a New York employer, he withholds New York State and City income taxes even though you only rehearsed in the Big Apple and then left for the provinces. If the show had lived long enough for you to play the Los Angeles and San Francisco engagements, he would have withheld yet an other tax: California state income tax. The New York State income tax would have been reduced by the amount of the California tax, but the New York City tax would have remained the same. Alas, however, Rosenkrantz and Polonius turned up missing in Phoenix and the rest of the tour had to be cancelled.

Note that in this example, as in the previous one, box 6 has been checked off at "Pension Plan." This is the union pension and *may* make you ineligible for an IRA deduction. This is not to say that you couldn't make an

IRA contribution that year, you just might not be able to *deduct* the contribution. (See Chapter 4.)

Note that box 10 is $105 greater than boxes 12 and 14 and that box 16 says: "L: 1785.00." In this example, you got a per diem of $630 per week or $90 per day. Let's say you played three weeks where the Federal per diem was only $85 per day. In this example you have exceeded that by $5 per day for 21 days, for a total of $105, so that excess is included in the amount in box 10. Read all that again and then ask yourself, "So what?" Here's what: you either account for the $1785 + $105 ($1890) by taking a deduction for travel or pay tax on the $105. Of course, if you are out on the road for a long time the amount of excess per diem reported can be substantial. As of this writing, Equity per diem is *not* more than the government rate for non-high cost locality.

1 Control number		OMB No. 1545-0008				
2 Employer's name, address, and ZIP code			6 Statutory employee ☐ Deceased ☐ Pension plan ☒ Legal rep ☐		942 emp ☐ Subtotal ☐ Deferred compensation ☐ Void ☐	
Residuals Distribution Centre 4599 Prairie Avenue Chicago, IL 30303			7 Allocated tips		8 Advance EIC payment	
			9 Federal income tax withheld 25.00		10 Wages, tips, other compensation 1012.50	
3 Employer's identification number 44-56565656565	4 Employer's state I.D. number		11 Social security tax withheld 124.00		12 Social security wages 1000.00	
5 Employee's social security number 987-65-4321			13 Social security tips		14 Medicare wages and tips 1000.00	
19 Employee's name, address, and ZIP code Ima Starr 945 West 55 Street NY, NY 10019			15 Medicare tax withheld 29.00		16 Nonqualified plans	
			17 See Instrs. for Box 17		18 Other Box 10 includes misc comp 12.50	
20	21		22 Dependent care benefits		23 Benefits included in Box 10	
24 State income tax 7.50	25 State wages, tips, etc. 1000.00	26 Name of state NY	27 Local income tax 1.30	28 Local wages, tips, etc 1000.00	29 Name of locality NYC	

Copy B To Be Filed With Employee's FEDERAL Tax Return   Department of the Treasury—Internal Revenue Service

Form **W-2 Wage and Tax Statement 1992** (Rev. 4-92)

This information is being furnished to the Internal Revenue Service.

Fig. 4

Figure 4 is the W-2 for your diaper commercial. Have a look at box 16. That $12.50 (excess over box 12 amount) is payment for wardrobe. Because you wore your own clothes, they've recompensed you an amount to cover the cost of cleaning. You should deduct this amount as "wardrobe maintenance." (See Chapter 5, "Miscellaneous Deductions . . .")

Notice also, please, that the withholding amounts are small in relation to the gross. You were afraid that they would take out too much and you needed the money, so you put down a bunch of *exemptions* on your W-4 when you did the gig. The commercial is national and running away, and you're making a bundle. You're going to be under-withheld in the following year. So contact the paymaster company and amend the W-4. You can amend a W-4 whenever you want. Change to an appropriate number of exemptions (see page 73). The following example requires *four* separate W-2 forms for only three jobs: a soap opera and two commercials. Certain large corporations produce a lot of soaps and commercials. They buy up a lot of afternoon time on TV.

In this example we see that three ad agencies that hired you have an account with the same sponsor: American Soap. KLOD Advertising (Figure 6) hired you for two days on a soap opera, Subliminal Concepts (Figure 7) used you in an ad for a deodorant, and Old and Gray (Figure 8) cast you in a commercial for cooking oil. The three ad agencies report wages and income taxes for the work you did for *them*. The sponsor reports Soc. Sec. for any and all work you did for any and all ad agencies or production companies they hire to do their good work. They don't want to overpay their share on your Soc. Sec. Before you can do your tax return, you have to make sure you have the "master" W-2 from Cincinnati (Figure 5), or wherever, as well as all the others from the agencies. You must make sure that box 10 on each of the forms from the ad agencies add up to the amount in box 12 or 14 on the master W- 2. If they do, then you've got them all.

If you find that the total of the various box 10s doesn't equal box 12 or 14 on the master W-2, then you may be missing a W-2, there may have been an error in someone's payroll department or the discrepancy may be wardrobe allowances. Check your pay stubs.

It will help to know how many jobs you've done in a year and for whom. You may remember the product, but not the name of the agency or production house. Write it on the list in Appendix I.

Oh, dear! Your unemployment ran out! You had to take a job waiting on tables. Your obligation as someone who earns tips is complicated and requires additional work on your part.

As a waiter, you report some of your tips to your employer and he withholds income tax and FICA on the wages he pays you and on the tips you report. You have to pay taxes on *all* the tips you make: you're required to keep a *daily* record of all your tips and a breakdown of how much you report to the employer and how much you don't.

I suggest you obtain, read, and use publication 1244 and forms 4070 and 4070-A therein. Then you'll know what you have to report to your employer, what you won't have to report, what you'll have to pay Social Security tax on and what you won't, and so forth. You can get this or any IRS publication by calling the IRS. Check your local listings.

If you work in Canada or get residuals from Canada, your earnings are reported on Form T-4 or NR-4. Just treat this the same as a W-2. You must report the money and pay tax on it, but, as you will eventually see, you can either deduct or take a *tax credit* for the Canadian tax or any foreign tax.

1 Control number		
	OMB No. 1545-0008	

6 Statutory employee ☐	Deceased ☐	Pension plan ☒	Legal rep. ☐	942 emp. ☐	Subtotal ☐	Deferred compensation ☐	Void ☐

2 Employer's name, address, and ZIP code

American Soap Folks
Cincinnati, OH

7 Allocated tips

8 Advance EIC payment

9 Federal income tax withheld

10 Wages, tips, other compensation

3 Employer's identification number	**4** Employer's state I.D. number
32-382436	

11 Social security tax withheld — 400.61

12 Social security wages — 3230.75

5 Employee's social security number
987-65-4321

13 Social security tips

14 Medicare wages and tips — 3230.75

19 Employee's name, address, and ZIP code

Ima Starr

15 Medicare tax withheld — 93.69

16 Nonqualified plans

17 See Instrs. for Box 17

18 Other

SOC SEC INFORMATION ONLY. OTHER W-2
INFO WILL BE REPORTED BY ADV AGENCY
(OUR SEC. 3504 AGENT

20 | **21** | **22** Dependent care benefits | **23** Benefits included in Box 10

24 State income tax	**25** State wages, tips, etc.	**26** Name of state	**27** Local income tax	**28** Local wages, tips, etc.	**29** Name of locality

Copy B To Be Filed With Employee's FEDERAL Tax Return   Department of the Treasury—Internal Revenue Service

Form **W-2 Wage and Tax Statement 1992** (Rev. 4-92)

This information is being furnished to the Internal Revenue Service.

Fig. 5

---

1 Control number		
	OMB No. 1545-0008	

6 Statutory employee ☐	Deceased ☐	Pension plan ☒	Legal rep. ☐	942 emp. ☐	Subtotal ☐	Deferred compensation ☐	Void ☐

2 Employer's name, address, and ZIP code

KLO'D Advertising, Inc.
Agents for American Soap
6666 Madison Avenue
NY, NY   10099

7 Allocated tips

8 Advance EIC payment

9 Federal income tax withheld — 136.10

10 Wages, tips, other compensation — 662.50

3 Employer's identification number	**4** Employer's state I.D. number
86-6943456	

11 Social security tax withheld

12 Social security wages

5 Employee's social security number
987-65-4321

13 Social security tips

14 Medicare wages and tips

19 Employee's name, address, and ZIP code

IMA STARR
945 West 55 St.
NY, NY   10019

15 Medicare tax withheld

16 Nonqualified plans

17 See Instrs. for Box 17

18 Other

NY SDI 1.20

20 | **21** | **22** Dependent care benefits | **23** Benefits included in Box 10

24 State income tax	**25** State wages, tips, etc.	**26** Name of state	**27** Local income tax	**28** Local wages, tips, etc.	**29** Name of locality
45.71	662.50	NY	14.39	662.50	NYC

Copy B To Be Filed With Employee's FEDERAL Tax Return   Department of the Treasury—Internal Revenue Service

Form **W-2 Wage and Tax Statement 1992** (Rev. 4-92)

This information is being furnished to the Internal Revenue Service.

Fig. 6

1 Control number			OMB No. 1545-0008								

2 Employer's name, address, and ZIP code	6 Statutory employee ☐	Deceased ☐	Pension plan ☒	Legal rep ☐	942 emp ☐	Subtotal ☐	Deferred compensation ☐	Void ☐

Holden Gray Advertising
Agents for American Soap
6666 Madison Avenue
NY, NY   10099

7 Allocated tips	8 Advance EIC payment

9 Federal income tax withheld 36.71	10 Wages, tips, other compensation 350.00

3 Employer's identification number 13-99696699	4 Employer's state I.D. number	11 Social security tax withheld	12 Social security wages

5 Employee's social security number 987-65-4321		13 Social security tips	14 Medicare wages and tips

19 Employee's name, address, and ZIP code	15 Medicare tax withheld	16 Nonqualified plans

Ima Starr
945 West 55
NY, NY   10019

17 See Instrs. for Box 17	18 Other NY SDI .60

20	21	22 Dependent care benefits	23 Benefits included in Box 10

24 State income tax 9.35	25 State wages, tips, etc. 350.00	26 Name of state NY	27 Local income tax 3.71	28 Local wages, tips, etc. 350.00	29 Name of locality NYC

Copy B To Be Filed With Employee's FEDERAL Tax Return   Department of the Treasury—Internal Revenue Service

Form **W-2 Wage and Tax Statement 1992** (Rev. 4-92)

This information is being furnished to the Internal Revenue Service.

Fig. 7

1 Control number			OMB No. 1545-0008								

2 Employer's name, address, and ZIP code	6 Statutory employee ☐	Deceased ☐	Pension plan ☒	Legal rep ☐	942 emp ☐	Subtotal ☐	Deferred compensation ☐	Void ☐

Subliminal Concepts, Inc.
Agent for American Soap
6666 Madison Avenue
NY NY   10099

7 Allocated tips	8 Advance EIC payment

9 Federal income tax withheld 303.08	10 Wages, tips, other compensation 2218.25

3 Employer's identification number 13-2899813	4 Employer's state I.D. number	11 Social security tax withheld	12 Social security wages

5 Employee's social security number 987-65-4321		13 Social security tips	14 Medicare wages and tips

19 Employee's name, address, and ZIP code	15 Medicare tax withheld	16 Nonqualified plans

Ima Starr
945 West 55 Street
NY NY   10019

17 See Instrs. for Box 17	18 Other NY SDI 3.90

20	21	22 Dependent care benefits	23 Benefits included in Box 10

24 State income tax 80.27	25 State wages, tips, etc. 2218.25	26 Name of state NY	27 Local income tax 29.83	28 Local wages, tips, etc. 2218.25	29 Name of locality NYC

Copy B To Be Filed With Employee's FEDERAL Tax Return   Department of the Treasury—Internal Revenue Service

Form **W-2 Wage and Tax Statement 1992** (Rev. 4-92)

This information is being furnished to the Internal Revenue Service.

Fig. 8

What records of earned income must a self-employed person keep?

You have to keep a set of books. They needn't be as complicated as a corporation's, but they must be accurate and comprehensible and show: 1) gross receipts (of money), and 2) disbursements (expenses). Anyone who pays you fees or commissions will report the money to IRS on a Form 1099-MISC and send a copy to you on or before the last day of February. Keep those 1099's. But suppose you want your tax return prepared before you get them? If you have *kept your own cash book of accounts received, you* can proceed, because *1099-MISC doesn't have to be attached to the return, unless there is an amount in box 4 and/or box 11.*

Figure 9 is a sample 1099-MISC:

☐ CORRECTED (if checked)

PAYER'S name, street address, city, state, and ZIP code		1 Rents $	OMB No. 1545-0115	**Miscellaneous Income**
Stage Theatre Fdtn, Inc. Suite 86, Heartbreak Hotel 55437462 Lonely Street Memphis, TN		2 Royalties $	1992	
		3 Prizes, awards, etc. $		
PAYER'S Federal identification number 45-67890123	RECIPIENT'S identification number 000-00-0000	4 Federal income tax withheld $	5 Fishing boat proceeds $	Copy B For Recipient
RECIPIENT'S name Chaim de Dazigne		6 Medical and health care payments $	7 Nonemployee compensation $ 2000.00	This is important tax information and is being furnished to the Internal Revenue Service. If you are required to file a return, a negligence
Street address (including apt. no.) 945 East 55th Street		8 Substitute payments in lieu of dividends or interest $	9 Payer made direct sales of $5,000 or more of consumer products to a buyer (recipient) for resale ▶ ☐	penalty or other sanction may be imposed on you if this
City, state, and ZIP code NY NY 10022		10 Crop insurance proceeds $	11 State income tax withheld $	income is taxable and the IRS determines that it has not been reported.
Account number (optional)		12 State/Payer's state number		

Form **1099-MISC**   (keep for your records)   Department of the Treasury - Internal Revenue Service

Fig. 4

There is no withholding from this kind of a payment because you're not a common law employee or an employee as defined for social security purposes. The money is most assuredly taxable, however.

Note to employees: Some producers report per diem on a 1099-MISC instead of on the W-2. So, if you are an employee, you *might* get a 1099-MISC sometimes, maybe.

If you receive commissions, author's royalties, or fees from anyone of $600 or more, that person or company is required to report the money to IRS and supply you with a copy of the form. If they pay you less than $600, the IRS excuses the payer from the work of filing the form. You, however, are not excused from paying tax on the money. And they might report it anyway. CAVEAT TAXEE.

Must a self-employed person pay estimated taxes?

You bet! Probably.

Just what are estimated taxes?

Since no employer is withholding and prepaying your income taxes or self-employment taxes, you must do it yourself. Using schedule ES, you estimate your gross receipts and expenses as a self-employed person and determine your "net" income. This amount is what you figure your self-employment tax on. Self-employment tax is an independent contractor's way of paying Social Security and Medicare taxes (FICA).

You then add your net income as a self-employed person to whatever other income you have—earned or nonearned—and subtract any estimated adjustments and deductions and exemptions that pertain, and you're ready to figure your estimated income tax. Add the income tax to the self-employment tax, divide by four, and you have the amount of your quarterly payments.

Quarterly, by the way, doesn't mean every three months to IRS. It means April 15, June 15, September 15, and January 15. You must save funds for estimated tax payments, and make them on time, or suffer penalties for underpayment. If you estimate you'll owe $500 or more, after reducing your liability by withholding tax and various credits, you must file. EXCEPTIONS: You needn't file if 1) you expect your withholding and tax credits to equal 90% or better of your final tax liability or 2) your withholding, credits, and other prepayments will equal 100% or better of your previous years' total tax liability.

Does an employee or someone who doesn't work at all ever have to pay estimated taxes?

Yes, on nonearned income, if it amounts to enough.

What are some examples of nonearned income and how is it reported?

Partnerships, estates and *trusts* report income (or loss) on *Schedule K-1.* You should get it on or before the due date of the entity's return. If you haven't received one by the time you go to get your taxes done, contact the appropriate accounting office for the partnership or estate and request the information. You do not have to attach a copy.

Like Forms 1099, there are many legal substitutes for Form K-1. Sometimes they are in the form of a letter. In the case of some tax shelters, they get very complicated with all kinds of information: where to report different amounts, tax liabilities to various states, and so on.

Unlike interest and dividend income, you probably don't have records elsewhere of the appropriate amounts to tell your tax person for partnership, estate, or trust income, so your return can really get delayed by missing partnership, rent, royalty* income, and information.

---

*There are two kinds of royalties: authors' royalties (subject to social security tax) and lease royalties (oil and gas).

If you sold property—such as stocks, bonds, your house—you will need all information pertinent to *the purchase* as well as the *sale* of the property. It would be efficient to check with your tax preparer, *before your appointment*, so that you'll know what information to have ready at that time.

One reason for keeping copies of old tax returns indefinitely is to be able to correctly report *taxable refunds*. Another is to prove by showing your career history that you are in it for the money and not just a hobby. Even if you haven't been doing too well, you can demonstrate "profit motive."

Code Section 183 bars using losses from an activity not engaged in for profit to offset income from other activities. They call an activity not engaged in for profit "a hobby". The "Hobby Loss Rule" assumes that an activity which shows a loss for three or more years is a hobby. This being the case, you are allowed to deduct expenses only up to the amount of income. How does this apply to you? I'll tell you how: Anyone in show business can have a bad run of luck. What is the state of the business right now as you read this? If you are making more money at the refreshment stand at the Lora Chase Musical Theatre than you are stage managing at the Lora Chase Musical Theatre, for example, and your total expenses applicable to stage managing are more than what you earned as a stage manager, you can't deduct them all thereby creating a loss and reducing the amount of your other income more than two years in a row. The Hobby Loss Rule is only a guideline the IRS uses and if they invoke it on you (disallowing ALL losses within a five year period which will cost you a bundle) you can appeal to tax court. If you do appeal to tax court you'd best be prepared to demonstrate profit motive and that there were some years when you made more money in the biz than you spent on staying in the biz. In other words, you made a profit sometimes and that at ALL times you tried to make a profit. As reported in the Research Institute of America's *Weekly Alert* of 4/27/95 Second Circuit Court: " . . . Code Sec. 183 isn't designed to punish the inept—only those who *deliberately* (emphasis added) engage in unprofitable activities and with a view to sheltering other income." I wonder if Second Circuit would include those who are hoping for that big break with the "inept"? Would the Court consider the state of the business during the years in question? Since the burden of proof is on you, the taxpayer, in these proceedings, you better save all your old tax returns and diaries to demonstrate profit motive and eptitude. Do they really think you take all those acting lessons and buy all those photographs etc., etc., to shelter the money you earn waiting on table?? Yes, that would be the assumption.

Those of you gentle readers who collect alimony have to report it as taxable income. No one sends you a form for it, so you have to keep track of this information yourself.

Since it's required that you keep an accounting of all taxable income, any other miscellaneous income that you may get should be noted by you in your diary or ledger.

Interest is reported on a Form 1099 INT. They generally don't mail you a form if your interest was under $10. But you are supposed to report it.

Since 1099 forms needn't be attached to your return, as long as you know what they will say, you can file your return without ever having received them.

There is one more source of money to talk about. It's a delicate subject, because it involves illegality. You've heard, perhaps, the expression "working off-the-books"? "Under the table"? Have you also heard the expression "the slammer"? Do you know the characteristic sound of metal bars clanging?

There are some people who do little gigs and are paid flat sums of money that they are told will not be reported. These lambs think that there is no record of their having received the money. Sometimes the people who pay them this money get audited by the IRS and the examiner will note a few names of recipients of small checks and send those names through to be audited. So you can get caught—er, rather *they* can get caught. The only kind of payment that cannot be traced from the payer is payment in currency.

The payee, on the other hand, is often very dumb. The payee often deposits these "off-the-books" payments in his or her checking account or savings account, where the IRS finds them. Why do people pay "off-the-books"? Because, by so doing, they avoid paying their share of your social security, unemployment, insurance premiums, Workmen's Compensation premiums, pension fund payments, and so on. They are not doing you a favor; they're doing themselves a favor and putting your neck on the chopping block at the same time. It's antisocial behavior, gang! It defeats everything the unions strive for. Use your head. Don't be a sucker. In more recent days, the expression "off-the-books" means merely: not on the payroll, which translates to: no taxes withheld, no benefits.

Some 1099's now have state or federal withholding taxes indicated. These SHOULD BE FILED WITH THE 1040.

2

Admissible Evidence
The Nature of Good Substantiation

As an artist, you have available to you a veritable cornucopia of legal write-offs. The reason for this is simple: Theatrical producers are in the business of making money. One way to make a profit is by keeping overhead low. Hence, producers pay as little as they can and let you pay for as much as possible. Expenses incurred doing business are deductible, so if your employer doesn't pay some expense of yours, you can deduct it, if you *can prove* you paid the expense, what the expense was, and demonstrate the necessity of the expense.

The majority of this book is taken up with what is deductible, but I feel the most important part is this section dealing with the nature of good substantiation of expenses. Since "the burden of proof is on the taxpayer," lend an ear!

The IRS doesn't have to take your word on anything. You need evidence of some kind for every deduction. Here are five forms of substantiation in more or less descending order of "weightiness":

1. Itemized bills marked "paid" for items paid in any manner.
2. Bills *and* canceled checks in payment.
3. Receipts and charge slips for credit card purchases.
4. Canceled checks.
5. Diary entries.

Paid Itemized Bills

The perfect substantiation! If a bill has your name, the date, a description of the item purchased or the service provided, and is marked "paid," you have proof positive. An IRS auditor could ask only for an explanation of the business purpose of the item or service. Alas, paid itemized bills are all too rare!

Bills and Canceled Checks

If you have a bill for something coaching, for example—and a canceled check that complements the bill in amount, proximity of time, name of creditor, and so forth, you have pretty good substantiation. A bill, by it-self, shows only that you owe somebody money for something. A com-plementary canceled check shows that you paid the bill. *A check, by itself, is worthless substantiation nine times out of ten.* Below are just two exam-ples that illustrate the weaknesses of a canceled check as substantiation of deductions.

1. You have a check made out to "Bob Otto." In the bottom left-hand corner of the check, you have annotated that the payment was for tap lessons. *No good!* Why? Because it's only your word. You can write whatever you want on the check. That serves only to help you remember what the check was for but is not proof. What can you do about this? Have Bob give you a receipt of payment. If he doesn't want to, get another coach. But, I know he'll give you a receipt. He's my pal.

2. A check paid to "The State of California." You have annotated that the check is in payment of taxes. Is the tax of the de-ductible kind? Is the amount all for tax or is part of it for penalty and/or interest? You should keep a copy of the *tax as-sessment.* That little piece of paper has the necessary explana-tion. Why is it necessary? Because a penalty is not deductible and tax and interest, which are, go to two different places.

A check to an individual is *never* good without a supporting bill or receipt of payment.

Can a canceled check by itself ever be accepted by the IRS?

Yes, some checks have enough information to demonstrate that it would be highly unlikely that the check was for a personal, nondeductible item. Some examples:

1. Checks to your unions for dues or initiation fees.
2. Checks paid to hospitals.
3. Blue Cross or some other health plan.
4. Checks to your church or temple.

There are more, but they are the exception rather than the rule. A check made to a "place"—a company or an institution—is more likely to be acceptable. A check to a person, never. "What, never?" "Well, hardly ever!"

One small moral point regarding paying with checks: If anyone asks you to make a check out to cash, it's almost certainly because he has no in-tention of passing the money "through the cash register." Pharmacists, doctors, coaches, anyone can do it. They cash those checks, live on the cash, and don't report it as income. They are cheating on their taxes. Why should you help them? We all end up paying for their share of the Pentagon. Does that thrill and delight you?

Receipts or Charge Slips for Cash Purchases

Receipts and charge slips are frequently lacking in hard information. The clerks often write simply "merchandise" on the charge slip or maybe an inventory control number. The date is sometimes incorrect. While a charge slip may have your name on it, cash-and-carry receipts seldom do. Cash register tapes have more faults than virtues. If the month and day are correct, they frequently lack the year. Three quarters of the time the date is incorrect. They might be printed faintly. They don't say what was purchased. And they definitely don't have your name on them.

What to do? It's simple! You improve on them. Correct the date, write your name down, write what was purchased, write why you purchased it, or write something that explains it. It's just too easy to save every receipt that passes through your hands all year and then arbitrarily decide that every penny you spent is deductible and then to write "makeup" on a receipt. So, the IRS is quite understandably skeptical about such substantiation.

Diary Entries

Diary entries for amounts spent on meals and incidental expenses (MIE), while traveling, and entertainment and incidental expenses while traveling or at home are acceptable substantiation for daily aggregate amounts up to $75 a day (as of 9/30/95).* The deductions themselves are dealt with in the appropriate chapters in this book.†

An acceptable diary entry is not cryptic. All the pertinent information is written clearly. Some short-hand is allowed, such as: MIE for meals and incidentals. Some examples:

1. "*Variety*, $1."
2. "Cocktails with Jon Jory, Director, Actors Theatre of Louisville. Discuss '96 '97 season. Sardi's $12.50, tip $1.80" ("Meeting with Jon" is *no good!*)
3. "Leave for Louisville. Cab to LaGuardia $9.50."
4. "Callback at Doyle, Dane for Bounty Comm. Cab going, $2.75; bus home, 50¢."
5. "Calling service, 60¢."
6. "To and from dentist, $1.50."
7. MIE $61.50 (while on the road).
8. Cab from rehearsal to special tap coaching with Bob Otto, $12.90.

---

*Reg §1.274-5T(c)(2)(iii)(B).
†Pay special attention to the subject of meals on the road later.

Besides substantiation of small cash expenditures, diaries are required and useful to prove that you actually work at being an artist, that you attempt to get work. In addition to an appointment book to use "in town," I strongly suggest that you use the travel and entertainment diary at the end of this book. Your best friend in an audit is your diary. The price is deductible, too. Who could ask for anything more?

Marcus Aurelius said:

> A diary is not just a good idea, it's a *requirement* of the Internal Revenue Code!

Brendan says:

> Even though you can throw your stuff out eventually (Federal statute is three years, in most states it is four), always keep a photocopy of your return, W-2 forms, and also your diary.

3

Organizing Yourself
Getting It Together and
Keeping It That Way

Getting all the necessary material for taxes organized is very difficult if you do it only once a year. You're asking for problems and I guarantee you'll find them. It's much easier if you develop a system and stick with it.

Diaries—"Mark me," Hamlet I, iv

I've already mentioned diaries. Let me repeat that I think you should have two—an appointment book and the expense diary in the back of this book. They are extremely helpful in reconstructing your activities during a year. And you may well have to reconstruct a year—for the IRS. A diary should be used daily or weekly and kept current. That way you don't have to rely on memory. Some folks bring their diaries up-to-date once a year. But, if you do this, you're running the risk of forgetting to put down some things, thereby cheating yourself out of some legitimate deductions.

Well-kept appointment books and travel diaries really help take the pain out of doing your taxes and can save your life in an audit. So, be sure you don't lose them, or your ticket to Paraguay.

Keeping Receipts and Checks

As you accumulate receipts and canceled checks, you should have a method of sorting and storing them. Two popular and easy ways I can recommend are:

> 1. *Accordion files.* I've always felt that the person who invented the accordion file should be given a Nobel Prize or a hickey. Accordion files can be labeled according to your individual needs, but you should make sure you get a generous enough one to enable you to avoid doubling up on the compartments. Browse your local stationery store. Any good office supply store should have a nice selection to choose from.
>
> Start off with a section for pay stubs, pay envelopes, W-2 forms, and so forth—anything having to do with income. The

rest of the sections should be used for the most common expenses—those which recur—with one section reserved for infrequent or one-time expenditures, like moving for business. In some instances you might double or triple up, viz: contributions, interest, taxes. On the other hand, you probably accumulate a lot of theatre ticket stubs so they would take an entire section in the file. You can always rearrange the file as you go along; so, label the sections in pencil. You will find after a few months what your particular needs are. My friend has a steel accordion file. He uses it to deflect bullets and shrapnel on the "A" train.

2. *Envelopes.* This method is just a variation on the accordion file. You label the envelopes instead of sections in the accordion file. There is a drawback to using envelopes: you can misplace one or more of them. So keep them in a shoe box or some other box. It's much harder to misplace a whole accordion file. On the other hand, if you need a new category, you just add an additional envelope to the collection. With the file, you may run out of sections and end up relabeling and juggling receipts around and doubling up. To each his own!

Whichever method you use, periodically sort out your accumulated receipts and canceled checks. I let them pile up on my dresser until my wife gets visibly irritated at the mess and then I sit down and sort them out into the accordion file. When I go to do my taxes every year, I have everything organized*

and the job is much easier. Your effects should be *sorted out by category, not by date—which is useless.*

Bookkeeping

Self-employed folks may have sufficient transactions to warrant keeping a set of books. Receipts and canceled checks verify the entries in the books. Artists who make a "product"—paintings, sculptures, or whatever—may have to take inventories. If you find the need to keep books and/or take inventories, I recommend you obtain and study *The Individual Artist: Record-Keeping, Methods of Accounting, Income and Itemized Deductions for Federal Income Tax Purposes* published and sold by Volunteer Lawyers for the Arts, 36 West 44th Street, New York, New York 10036.

In general, self-employed people need only be able to separate expenses connected with self-employment from any they may incur as an occasional employee. Both employees and self-employed persons need to separate business from "nonbusiness" deductions.

*A BIG FAT LIE!

4

Adjustments to Income

Certain expenses may be subtracted from gross income. They are called Adjustments to Income.

- Payments to individual retirement accounts (IRAs)
- Moving Expense
- 1/2 of self-employment tax
- Self-employed health insurance deduction
- Payments to Keogh and SEP plans
- Penalty on early withdrawal of savings
- Alimony payments
- Qualified Performing Artist deduction (QPA)

The really nice thing about adjustments is that the amounts can be *subtracted* from *gross income* and you can still take a standard deduction—which is the option you take if your itemized deductions (discussed further along) are not more than the standard deduction applicable to you. The really nasty thing about Congress is that they have made all travel expense a Miscellaneous Deduction on Schedule A. What this means is that all you can do is wipe out any erroneously reported per diem with your W-2 earnings. After you subtract adjustments, you have the figure known as the "Adjusted Gross Income" or "AGI" in the trade. Remember the term! I'll be using it later.

Payments to an Individual Retirement Arrangement

If you are an employee (self-employeds see "Keogh Plans," below), you can start your own retirement account and deduct your contributions to it even if you participate in an employer's pension plan or a union retirement fund. The deduction amount limitation is the smaller of either: (1) $2,000, or (2) 100 percent of your annual earned income.

If you contribute to a so-called "employer-sponsored plan" or government plan and your payments to it are qualified voluntary contributions, you may deduct those contributions to the extent of the limitations noted above. If you also have your own independently owned IRA, your deductions to it may not exceed the dollar limitation when combined with your voluntary contributions to the employer-sponsored plan or government plan.

For spousal IRAs, the dollar limitation is raised to $2,250. The contributions can be divided between the two IRAs in any manner as long as not more than $2,000 is contributed to either. Also, a joint return must be filed in order to take a deduction for a spousal IRA. Divorced persons may continue a spousal IRA under certain conditions. CWYTP!

If you are covered by an employer's retirement plan (and almost any performing union job is covered, the exceptions being some "small" Equity jobs and SAG, up to a point. Beware SAG extra work! Your W-2 will have the pension box checked off, but you may not have earned enough to really have had a contribution made. If that's the only union work you got and you are otherwise eligible to deduct an IRA contribution, you should obtain a letter from SAG Pension Fund stating that you were not a participant for that year and attach it to your return. Otherwise the IRS will adjust your return and set you an unpleasant letter), your eligibility begins to phase out after your earnings (as modified to "modified adjusted gross

FROM FORM 8606

If you (or your spouse if filing a joint return) were COVERED by a retirement plan and—

you checked Filing Status box:	and your modified AGI* is:	you:
1 or 4 on Form 1040, page 1	$25,000 or less	Can take a full IRA deduction (use Worksheet 1)
	Over $25,000 but less than $35,000	Can take a partial IRA deduction (use Worksheet 2)
	$35,000 or more	Cannot take an IRA deduction (see Nondeductible Contributions)
2 or 5 on Form 1040, page 1	$40,000 or less	Can take a full IRA deduction (use Worksheet 1)
	Over $40,000 but less than $50,000	Can take a partial IRA deduction (use Worksheet 2)
	$50,000 or more	Cannot take an IRA deduction (see Nondeductible Contributions)
3 on Form 1040, page 1	Over $-0- but less than $10,000	Can take a partial IRA deduction (use Worksheet 2)
	$10,000 or more	Cannot take an IRA deduction (see Nondeductible Contributions)

Modified AGI (adjusted gross income) is the amount on Form 1040, line 22, minus the total of any deductions claimed on Form 1040, lines 23, 25 through 28, and any write-in amount included on line 29.

Fig. 10

income," or "modified AGI") reach a certain amount. Refer to Figure 10, which is a chart reproduced from the 1987 1040 instruction booklet.

1997 Tax Act Changes

Beginning in 1998, the limitation "windows" (see Fig. 10) begin to rise each year until, in 2005, it goes from $50,000-$60,000 for single taxpayers and, in 2007, it goes to $80,000-$100,000 for married couples filing jointly.

Good news! Starting in 1998, if one spouse is covered by a qualified employer plan *and the other one isn't*, they can now make a deductible contribution for the uncovered partner. The contribution phases out when the combined AGI falls between $150,000 and $160,000.

Beginning in 1998, you can make withdrawals from your IRA without penalty if:

you use the money (up to a $10,000 lifetime limitation) for death or disability, first-time home purchase (you are a "first-time" home buyer if you have not owned a principle residence during the twenty-four months prior to the date of the Purchase and Sale agreement or commencement of construction if you are building that little bungalow;

you use the money to pay higher education costs for yourself, spouse, children, step-children, grandchildren, or step-grandchildren.

Beginning in 1998, you can, subject to phase-out, contribute and deduct up to $500 per year to an **education IRA** to pay the higher education expenses of a person designated by you.

Beginning in 1998 you can start a *Roth IRA*. Roth contributions are not deductible on your tax return; but, with certain restrictions, withdrawals are entirely tax free. The maximum contribution, based on your *earned* income, is $2000 (less any contributions to a regular IRA in the same year). Whereas in the case of a regular IRA you can't make contributions after age 70½ , you can make Roth contributions after that age.

Some Roth restrictions:

Single filers "phase-out": $95,000-$110,000
Married-filing-jointly "phase-out": combined AGI $150,000-$160,000
Married filing separately: no contribution allowed

Withdrawals are tax free if:

the money was in the Roth for five years;
you are 59½ years old at the time (except in the case of death or
disability or if you are a first time home buyer).

You can roll over a regular IRA into a Roth IRA. If your AGI is over
$100,000, however, the amount of the rollover is treated as income and
included in taxable income pro-rated over four years, BUT without the 10%
penalty usually imposed on early withdrawals from IRA's.

If you are partly or completely ineligible to deduct an IRA contribution,
you may want to shelter some of the earnings of your savings by making a
nondeductible contribution. To do this you would use and file Form 8606
with your tax returns.

The contribution to the IRA must be in money, not property. If you contribute more than your limitation in any year, you can avoid the 6 percent
excise tax on excess contributions by withdrawing the excess amount before
the due date of your return for that year (April 15 in most cases). You should
know by April 15 of any year how much money you earned the year before.
Automatic extensions of filing date include extension of time to make IRA
contributions or withdrawals of excess contributions.

Moving Expenses

You may deduct reasonable moving expenses if you relocate for a new job. In
order to qualify for the deduction, the distance from your *old residence* to
your new business location has to exceed the distance from your *old residence*
to your *old business* location by 50 miles. Also, you have to work 39 weeks
out of the 12 months following the move or 78 weeks out of the 24 months
following the move (with not less than 39 weeks during the first 12 of the 24
months). By "work" they mean full-time employment or self-employment.
You can, however, disregard this requirement if employment ends because of
death, disability, involuntary separation, or transfer for your employer's benefit. If you have not satisfied the 39-week requirement by the end of a calendar
year, but think you will in the next year, you can take the deduction anyway.
But if you don't make it in the next year, you're supposed to declare an
amount equal to the deduction as *income* in the next year.

Of course, in show business, "involuntary separation" occurs all the
time. It's the nature of the work. If you move frequently, the IRS will call
you an itinerant—oh, gypsy—and not allow any of it.

Moving expenses must be explained on IRS Form 3903 (transportation
and lodging, for one trip only, but *no meals*). Lodging in your old location
for *one* night may be deducted, if you're out of your house or apartment

because your furniture is gone, as well as lodging for *one* night in the new location while waiting to move in.

To prove the deducted amounts, save receipts from the mover, trains, planes, lodging, and tolls. If you drive, note the mileage in your diary. Local public transportation should also be noted in your diary. You have the option of deducting actual out-of-pocket expenses for gasoline, oil, repairs, and so forth during the move, or the standard allowance, whichever is greater.

Self-Employment Tax

Designers, writers, and other self-employed folks can deduct one-half of your self-employment tax computed on your net income on Schedule SE. Neat, huh?

Self-Employed Health Insurance Deduction

Any self-employed person who has a net profit and was not eligible to participate in a subsidized health plan of an employer (other than yourself) or an employer of your spouse's may be able to take a deduction for up to 30 percent of health insurance premiums. The amount is limited to a percentage of premiums paid or your net profit, whichever is less. If you have employees, you cannot take the deduction unless you have provided the same health insurance for them.

Limitation:

1997	=	40%
1998-99	=	45%
2000-01	=	50%
2002	=	60%
2003-05	=	80%
2006	=	90%
2007	=	100%

Payments to Keogh and SEP Retirement Accounts

Self-employed folk, folks who work for flat fees and not on salary, can also have their own "pension" plan, under the provisions of HR 10.

There are several prototype plans which are legal, depending on whether you have employees, but the most common arrangement for an individual is a

so-called "defined contribution" plan. In plain language, it means you can contribute and deduct a percentage of your "net," your profit from business

The maximum contribution is 15 percent of net earnings as adjusted, with
a ceiling of $30,000. Net earnings from self-employment are the "owner's
compensation," and it is this figure on which the contribution is based after an
adjustment for the amount to be contributed is made. Does that sound like one
of Sartre's "whirligigs"? How can you know what you can deduct if you have
to know what you can deduct in order to figure out what you can deduct?
(Sounds like the Sanity Clause!) Rest easy, dear reader; just multiply your net
from self-employment by 13.0435 percent. A magic figure! Just like π. A
piece of cake! Wait a minute! How can π be cake? (Definitely, Chico should
get these lines.) For "Defined Benefit" plans and SEP plans the percentage is
different. Consult with your investment counselor.

The idea of Keoghs,, SEPS, and indeed IRAs is to defer taxes on a portion of your income until your retirement or age 59½—whichever is later—
but no later than age 70½, when you will be (presumably) in a lower tax
bracket. We should all live so long! Automatic extensions of filing date also
include extension of time to make Keogh and SEP contributions.

Penalty on Early Withdrawal of Savings

You know those savings accounts where you give them a lump of money,
say $1,000, for a specified time, say a year, and they give you a nonstick
casserole and a little higher interest than an ordinary savings account? These
are savings certificates, nest eggs, CDs, time accounts—they go by various
names, depending on which ad agency the bank uses. Well, if you take the
money out before the time you agreed on is up, the bank penalizes you by
keeping some money while declaring the whole amount of interest to the
government. You can write off, on your return, the amount of penalty for
pulling out too soon. You get an "adjustment to income" and you can *keep*
the *nonstick casserole!*

Alimony Payments and Separate Maintenance

Alimony or separate maintenance payments are deductible if you are
divorced or legally separated and the payments are required, paid in dis-
charge of a legal obligation, paid after the decree, and paid periodically. But
. . . you can't file a joint return with your ax-spouse!

Don't confuse alimony with child support, which is not deductible but
may mean you can claim dependent exemptions for the children. Alimony
recipients, be aware that you have to pay income tax on alimony and may
have to file estimated taxes. Payments made under a decree entered before

March 2, 1954, are not deductible, but they're also not taxable to the recipient.

You must write in your ax-spouse's social security number on the front of the 1040 where requested. You may be surprised that an ex-spouse won't return your calls sometimes and it's April 14 and your preparer is having a breakdown. If you can't get the number, attach a note to your 1040 saying he or she wouldn't give it to you. See if anything happens.

Reimbursed Employee Business Expense (R.E.)

If you get per diem from an employer and it is less than the government amount, it is not supposed to be reported on your W-2 or on a 1099-MISC. *If it is*, however, IRS says you can get rid of it by writing "R.E." on the 1040 on the line after "Alimony" in the space to the left of the column and including the amount in the total on line 30.

If your employer is *not* reporting the per diem, your choices are:
1. If you spent pretty much just what you received, it's a wash and you can ignore it and not bother to deduct expenses.
2. If you spent more than the per diem (which is usually the case), you'll want to write off the "excess expenses." Form 2106 is designed to take care of these expenses and per diems. This form as well as the expenses and treatment of unreported per diem payments are discussed later in the section treating Employee Business Expenses subject to 2% of AGI limit.

QPA

Remember "AGI"? Well, Sir, compute 2% of it and subtract that from the total of your professional expenses—travel, entertainment, and all your miscellaneous deductions!

Congress figured since the standard deduction was increased and the personal exemption was increased generously (in their opinion), it was fair to impose a percentage floor on miscellaneous deductions. They giveth it and they sticketh it and we geteth it and it hurteth; if we don't geteth political and writeth some letters we becometh as sheep. We all know what happens to sheep every April 15: fleeced!

But thanks to the Actors' Equity Association and Stage Source in Boston (among several concerned organizations), and a lot of individuals' hard work, a provision was written into the 1986 Tax Act that gave a measure of relief for *certain* performing artists. If you meet the qualifications of the provision, you can write off *all* your business expenses on page one of Form 1040 as an adjustment to income, reducing the total of those expenses *only* by any reimbursement you may have received and irrespective of a percentage floor. Here are the qualifications:

You must be an individual who has performed services for at least two employers in the performing arts (this would seem to include support personnel) during the year in question; your legal deductions connected with performing said services must equal more than 10 percent of gross income from performing arts (not 10 percent, *more* than 10 percent); your adjusted gross income, without taking the performing arts deductions into account, must be $16,000 or less.

Read it through a few times. If you stop to think about that 2 percent floor, you might get mad enough to do something about it. Consider: The average working stiff may have some union dues and maybe some unreimbursed uniform and small tools amounting to a few hundred dollars a year, so maybe the increased standard deduction and exemption does make up for the lost 2 percent. But what if you have a good year—say $100,000 (not so uncommon these days. The last couple of years, some of the returns I've been doing look as if I was writing down fire) you lose $2,000 on Schedule A (.02 x 100,000). I think we could use a "dollar cap" on the 2 percent floor or some special-interest legislation for salaried-cum-self-employed freelance professionals. Written to your congresspersons lately?

On April 28, 1993, at the instigation of Actor's Equity Association, the subject of tax reform was discussed at a meeting of the Department for Professional Employees. Present were representatives and members (this writer included) of AEA, SAG, AFTRA, AGMA, AGVA, IATSE, & AFM. SAG's legal counsel and lobbyists present opined that to try for Statutory Employees status for performers would be opening Pandora's Box at this time with this Congress. I had suggested to Equity's Legislative Committee at a previous meeting on April 6, 1993 that we should get the dollar limit on Qualified Performing Artists (see: pg vii) eliminated or raised because doing so would accomplish the same goal as Statutory Employees status. At the April 28 meeting, opinion also was expressed that we ask for other restrictions to be eased so that the "QPA" provision benefit a greater number of taxpaying artists and support personnel. If you belong to any of the above mentioned unions, I urge you to urge them to try for no limit or a very high limit on earnings and elimination of the two-employer and the joint-income requirement. This will grant you all PARITY with truly self-employed people and this is nothing less than fair.

As of October 15, 1993, this issue did not make it into the *Revenue Reconciliation Act of 1993*. It remains to be seen if it gets into any other tax bill such as a technical corrections act. Write some letters!!

1996 UPDATE: I guess you didn't write any letters because *ten years later*, the QPA income limit is still $16,000 and no one has been able to do anything about it. After the April '93 meeting, Equity paid a huge sum of money to SAG's lawyers to go down to Washington and make the attempt described above. They were told to buzz off! And they did. We should have sent some sexy celebrities. Why is it these movie stars and Broadway stars will go down to Washington and testify for every damn cause except their own concerns? Could it be because they never been asked to? I'd ask them only I don't know any of them. Of course, as "loan-out corporations" these laws don't effect them anyway. Here is the Treasury Department's response to the efforts as extracted from "The Statement of Leslie B. Samuels, Assistant Secretary (Tax Policy), Department of the Treasury before the Subcommittee on Select Revenue Measures of the House Committee on Ways and Means," a press release of September 21, 1993:

"... E. INDIVIDUAL INCOME TAX.

1. *Increase Eligible Income Level for Performing Artist Employee Exemption from the Limitation on Deduction for Unreimbursed Business Expenses.*

Administration position. Do not support. Present law provides a deduction in computing adjusted gross income (and thereby also an exemption from the 2-percent floor on miscellaneous itemized deductions) for a limited class of low-income performing artists. We are unaware (emphasis added) *of any justification for expanding this relief* by more than doubling the income limitation ..."

What about taking a real look at the cost of living in New York or Los Angeles and reminding yourself that the $16,000 limitation applies to married couples as well as single taxpayers??? What about CPI and Cost-of-living adjustments to the amount? Hmmm? The Author wants to know! Wouldn't you like to know? It's ten years later, for God's sake! Would somebody out there go to an Equity or SAG meeting and ask the damn leadership, the Executive Director or the Treasurer or the President or the First Vice-President why the only time they try to do something is when I nag them? Why isn't Paul or Clint or Whoopie helping out? Will someone ask one of them to help? The union leadership isn't going to try to enlist their help. They're not reading this book, you are. So, you ask them. Ask Jerry Lewis. He'd be good. Or Charlton or Al or Dustin or Jay or Dave or Zelda. Creighton Barrow would go, but he can't get the fare together.

5

Deductions

Now that we have arrived at your adjusted gross income, we are faced with the decision to itemize or not to itemize. It's an easy decision to make: whichever means the lower taxable income is the way to go. You simply have to add up all your itemized deductions and compare the total with whichever standard deduction applies to you. For example, let's say you're sixty, sighted, and single. Your standard deduction is $3,900 (for 1995) and your itemized deductions add up to $4,410. You file the itemized. The greater your deductions, the lower your taxable income is. The lower your taxable income is, the lower your tax is. The lower your tax is, the happier you are.

Itemized deductions are:

- Medical and dental
- Taxes you paid
- Interest you paid
- Contributions you made
- Casualty and theft losses
- Miscellaneous deductions subject to 2 percent AGI limit
- Other miscellaneous deductions

Medical Deductions

Any money you spend to diagnose, mitigate, prevent, alleviate, or correct an illness of body or mind is deductible. Expenses to maintain good health are not deductible. For example, vitamins are not deductible.

You should understand that some medical expenses are mistaken to be professional expenses: capping of teeth and so forth. You may be prompted by professional reasons to obtain treatment of this kind, but these items must be deducted as medical expenses, and the amounts paid are subject to the percentage restrictions discussed below.

Treatment or procedures need not be performed by a licensed person as long as the treatment or operation is a legal one, viz: treatment at a commercial establishment for baldness, if the baldness is *because of a disease.* The fact that you may be a performer has no bearing on the deductibility of the expense. The fact that the person treating you at Schwartz's Hair Studio is not a dermatologist also has no bearing on the deductibility. (Is the disappearance of your locks inherited? For the disappearance of your lox, see "Roommates, Inconsiderate.")

Here is a checklist of common allowable medical deductions:

- Health and contact lens insurance (Self-employed people, see Adjustments to Income)
- Prescriptions, medicines, and contact lens equipment and supplies
- Special foods for hypertense or hypoglycemic folks *may* be. CWYTP.
- M.D.s
- Dentists (caps are for chewing, not getting work)
- Chiropractors
- Eye doctors and subsequent optical expense for purposes of looking at the world. Lenses are not a professional deduction. They're so you can find your soup . . . or your glasses.
- Nursing care
- Labs, clinics, etc.
- Ambulance fees
- Support hose
- Transportation to and from treatment (even out-of-town, if the treatment is not available where you are). Diary for local fares!
- Psychiatric care by any qualified person or place. Psychologists are deductible. On the other hand, gurus, spiritual advisors, and folks who take your money and then yell at you all weekend may be giving you a lesson in life, but it won't wash at the IRS.
- Equipment such as air conditioners, amplification for your phone, and elevators may be deducted or capitalized. CWYTP!
- Physical exams
- Telephone calls to psychologist

Here is a list of some of the things that have been tried and panned:

- Diaper service
- Getting buried
- Marriage counseling
- Reducing treatments
- Fallout shelters
- Golf
- Health club membership
- Cosmetic surgery (except to correct congenital or other deformity

The list of the "cans" and the "cannots" is extensive. Just remember: *When in doubt, get a receipt.*

Regarding insurance . . . you may or may not have any. Depending on your union, you may get coverage while you're working and for a period after the show closes, or for a whole year when you have earned a certain amount. Check with your union. If you are allowed to continue coverage on your own after a show closes, I recommend that you do so.

Here's how the medical deduction works: You keep good records of what you pay. Keep whatever statements come with the checks from the insurance company for reimbursements. From what you paid out, you subtract what you got back, add in all other legal medical expenses, then subtract 7.5 percent of AGI. Tee hee! Congress got you again.

Keep in mind that a medical expense is deductible in the year that it's *paid,* not the year in which the service was performed. CWYTP as to whether you should postpone paying for treatments until a subsequent year. Because of the 7 1/2 percent "floor," you can distribute payments on your medical expenses over two years and not get a deduction in either. It sounds crazy, but if you're having a bad year, try to get medical bills paid off before December 31. You'll get a bigger deduction. If you've had a good year, see if the Doc will wait till after January 1. Next year might be a poor year.

Never pay in one year for treatment to be received in the following year. It isn't deductible!

PROOF: Bills and canceled checks and/or receipts for payment.

Interest

The Tax Code defines two kinds of interest: personal interest and mortgage interest. Personal interest isn't deductible anywhere. *What is personal interest?* Any legal interest that isn't mortgage interest. What's illegal interest? Don't ask! Mortgage interest is still fully deductible on a principal residence and a second home to the extent that the amount borrowed doesn't exceed the cost of the home plus improvements. If the interest on an excess borrowed amount is spent on medical or educational expense, it, too, is deductible. If not, it's deemed personal interest.

Self-employed folks note that interest on a business loan or credit card or charge purchases is deductible as a business expense on Schedule C.

PROOF: Statements from lenders disclosing interest paid during the year.

Taxes

The only deductible taxes you must keep records of are the ones for which you are billed such as real estate, personal property taxes, additional income taxes for prior years billed to you and paid during the current year. Deductible state and local income taxes are already on your W-2 form.

Residents of California, New York, New Jersey, and Rhode Island can deduct payments to State Disability Insurance, but not payments to private plans which replace "Salary."

PROOF: Assessments and canceled checks, W-2 forms.

Contributions

Any money, property, or goods donated to a recognized religious organization, qualified charity, or not-for-profit corporation is deductible. Donations to needy individuals don't count. If you go to church and put more than two dollars a week in the collection, write out a check or use the church's envelopes if they have them. The IRS is justifiably suspicious of claims of currency in the collection plate. If you donate more than $250 at one swell foop to any charity, you must obtain contemporaneous written proof from them before you file your return.

If someone comes to your door, collecting for one of the charities, make them show an I.D. They have them, if they're legitimate. They also are issued blank receipts to fill out if you give cash. Always try to make cash contributions with a check rather than currency. Contributions other than cash fall into two categories:

1. **Your time**
   You *cannot* evaluate your time and deduct it. You *can*, however, deduct out-of-pocket expenses connected with donating your time to a charity or nonprofit organization. If you use your car, deduct the current mileage allowance or actual out-of-pocket expense, whichever is more!

2. **Goods and property**
   a. If you donate clothes or goods you need an evaluation and receipt for the goods from the organization to attach to your return. (See Appendix I.) Some charities do not evaluate donated goods. So, if you plan to deduct, before you make the donation make sure the organization will give you an evaluation. If over $500, you must complete and attach Form 8283. CWYTP.
   b. Property—real and otherwise. If you have stocks, land, or any other income-producing property you want to give to charity, CWYTP! This is a complicated form of deduction and you should get professional counsel.

You can take deductions for contributions up to an amount equal to 50 percent of your adjusted gross income. If your donations exceed this figure, you can carry the excess over to a succeeding year.

If you buy something at a thrift store, a raffle ticket for the benefit of a church, or a sale, you may not be able to deduct anything or, at best, part of what you pay, viz: you pay $20 for an Actors' Fund Benefit. You're sitting in what is ordinarily an eight-dollar seat. You have a twelve-dollar deduction. If you buy a kitchen table at a thrift store, you have no deduction. You've received something for your money.

Block association dues usually are deductible. Money earmarked for a block guard usually is not. Check with your block association.

Gifts of art come under close scrutiny, so get a good, qualified appraisal. Artists donating your own art, CWYTP.

Remember, with the exception of agents, it is better to give than to receive.

Casualty and Theft Losses

For tax purposes, *theft* covers, but is not limited to, larceny, robbery, and embezzlement. It's when someone illegally deprives you of your property. Of course, you have to be able to prove you were ripped off. So, report all thefts to the boys in blue. The IRS would like you to be able to prove you owned the property stolen, so you should hang onto receipts for TVs, recorders, typewriters, good jewelry, furs, and so on. If something was given to you or is an heirloom, you may have trouble proving you ever had it, let alone proving its value. Sometimes the IRS has accepted affidavits from third parties. If you are audited on a theft loss and have to pay for a copy of the police report, that payment is deductible.

The amount to be deducted is the *resale value* of the stolen items or purchase price, whichever is less. Clothing, except for furs, has practically no resale value at all. Good jewelry, furs, art, good musical instruments—anything that appreciates in value over the years—can be deducted at purchase price. It needn't be depreciated. After figuring the resale price of the gone goods, you have to subtract what your insurance, if any, paid and then $100 for Uncle Sam. What's left over may be your deduction. If there *is* anything left over. Good locks and window gates are not deductible, but they are a great investment if you go on the road. Each separate loss must exceed $100 and the total amount of deductible losses during the year must exceed 10 percent of AGI.

A casualty loss is the destruction of property by an identifiable event like a fire or flood. There is no case history I know of regarding claims for poltergeist damage. Things like gradual erosion, termite damage, or rats eating your camper have been denied by IRS. As far as determining the amount to be deducted for casualty loss, I have little to say here, except CWYTP! It's far too technical and complicated to detail in this modest missal. There's that echo again: "CWYTP!"

Miscellaneous Deductions Subject to 2 Percent AGI Limit

This includes just about everything else ever allowed by the IRS. In the Introduction, in regard to getting too detailed in this book, I said ". . . you might as well reproduce the Internal Revenue Code." Well, I'm going to give you a little of it: the beginning of Code Section 162. You will appreciate, even if you have but a tither of imagination, that the words "ordinary and necessary expenses" open Pandora's box. It has led to more litigation than even Giles Corey could have imagined in his wildest dreams. (What do you mean, you don't know who Giles Corey is? He gets to utter that delicious line in Arthur Miller's *The Crucible,* "A fart on Thomas Putnam!").

> **Sec. 162. Trade or business expenses.**
> **(a) In General.**
> There shall be allowed as a deduction all the ordinary and necessary expenses paid or incurred during the taxable year in carrying on any trade or business, including . . .
>
> **(2)** traveling expenses (including amounts expended for meals and lodging other than amounts which are lavish or extravagant under the circumstances) while away from home in the pursuit of a trade or business . . .

The subsection "In General" has been specified, broadened, narrowed, and generalized by innumerable court cases and Treasury regulations. In the listing that follows, I cite Section 162 only when I find nothing more specific in addition to 162. These citations are bases for taking deductions, *in my opinion,* and do not necessarily reflect the views of this station, God, or the IRS. The less specific the citation (Section 162 or the Cohan Rule), the more disputatious an audit examiner is likely to be. I will get into disputatiousness in the chapter on audit examinations.

The proper citation of the Cohan Rule is: *Cohan* v. *Com.,* (1932, CA2) 39 F2d 540. It says in main that a taxpayer *may* be able to deduct an estimated amount even if his other records or proof are not adequate to substantiate the expenditure. The expense has to meet the standards of "ordinary and necessary" and must be reasonable in type and amount. Of course, since 1932, when dear old George M. tilted with the Commissioner, endless statutes, regulations, and court cases have narrowed the application of Cohan to almost nothing. The most stunning blow in recent times is the optional standard daily meal allowance in place of an estimate. I've often said and probably my last words will be: "If you're too stupid or lazy to write in a diary, you deserve $9 per day for meals!" (In what film did what character say to John Wayne, as he gazed at the sign over a pub door, "Over here, we pronounce it: ko-HAN"? What actor played the part? Clue: His real name was Louis Shields.)

Here's a sampling of the results of some "ordinary and necessary" court cases:

> *Wilson,* 49 TC 406 . . . an expense can be considered nonrelated at one time and at another time be deemed absolutely ordinary and necessary.
>
> *Welch* v. *Helvering,* 290 US 111, 78 L Ed 212 . . . an expense is ordinary if its use is customary in the taxpayer's trade or business . . . the courts may accept as what is necessary those expenses deemed so in the taxpayer's judgment.
>
> *Dannemiller, Walter J.,* TC Memo 1958-105 . . . an expense was disallowed because the Tax Court found it was not customary to the taxpayer's business.
>
> *Poletti, Madyo A.* v. *Com.* (1964, CA8) 330 F2d 818 . . . The Eighth Circuit rejects Dannemiller as discouraging to innovation and ingenuity and holds that an expense does not have to be usual as long as the taxpayer can establish the expense is reasonably connected to his business.

These cases specify "ordinary and necessary." In Fisher, 23 TC 218, which has to do with deducting wardrobe (in this case a musician's tuxedo and accessories), the IRS seems to have found an armor-piercing principle used in attacking deductions for makeup and dance wear. They seem to feel that while an expense may be ordinary and necessary to a trade or profession if it is adaptable to personal use or suitable to personal use, you can't deduct it. I can't understand why they haven't extended the principle to include postage stamps, stationery, work boots, and pencil sharpeners. Everything that's ordinary and necessary. "How do I know you didn't buy those tickets to your show for that casting director just because it made you feel good?" "How do I know you don't get out that sheet music and sing those songs sometimes at a party? Huh?" There'll be more on this as we go along.

I'll confine my efforts, as I have said elsewhere, to those items deductible if you are in the "biz," although others may find goodies lurking here. I'll indicate in parentheses what sort of substantiation is required for each deduction and in brackets an authority for deducting it. *Let me remind freelancers that this sea of deductions we are about to launch into may be, indeed probably* is, *made up of business expenses for you, to be written off on your self-employment schedule.* CWYTP.

Here goes:

1. Initiation fees and dues to professional unions and societies. (Bills and checks). [REV RUL 69-214, 1969-1 CB 52]
2. Contract legal fees. (Bills and checks) [Code Sec. 162]
3. Commissions to agents and managers. (Bills and checks) [Reg. § 1.461-1(a)(1)]
4. Professional registries: Players Guide, Academy Players, Role Call, Funny Face, etc. (Bills and checks) [Reg. § 1.162-1.]
5. Classes, coaching lessons. (As long as they maintain and improve the skills of your profession. They're not allowable if they prepare you for another line of work.) In an audit, an examiner will usually ask you to get verification from a coach if the checks are made out to his name. Get a bill from the coach. (Bills and checks) [Reg. § 1.162-6]
6. Cosmetics and dressing-room supplies for professional use. This does not include street makeup, or what you use for going to auditions, but does include makeup for showcases. Some IRS examiners want to disallow all makeup. What they don't know is that lighting being what it is these days, you don't need to use the values or types of makeup such as grease paint. More and more ordinary street hues are suitable. How do they figure that should mean you shouldn't be allowed to deduct it? They allowed an assistant district attorney to deduct a tape recorder. He swore it was not used for personal music listening. So, if they disallow your makeup, say, "I cross my heart, hope to die, and a cellar full of rats, I don't, I swear, I don't use this makeup on dates." It may not do any good, though. (Receipts—write the name of the show on the receipt.) [Code Sec. 162]
7. Hair care. This must be for a specific *job,* not general, looking-for-work upkeep. I recommend that if a director wants you to change hairstyle or color, and isn't going to pay for it, ask to have a rider in your contract stating that the "actor will maintain hairstyle at his own expense." That way, you'll get by in an audit. (Receipts and checks) [Code Sec. 162]
8. Photographs and resumes. This includes production shots. (Bills and checks) [Reg. § 1.162-1]
9. Stationery and postage for mailing resumes, business correspondence. Diaries, staples, stapler, etc. (Bills, checks, and receipts) [Code Sec. 162, Reg. § 1.162-6; TC Memo 4/1/46, 15 TCM 570.]
10. Theatre books, scripts, scores, sheet music, strings, rosin, picks, batteries for cassette recorders, tapes, records, etc. (Bills, checks, and receipts) [Code Sec. 162; Reg. § 1.162-6]

11. a. A portion of your home telephone for business but not the *base monthly* rate on your first line, not even a portion of it. You can deduct 100 percent of a second line or of your business phone, if you have one. If you have a roommate, the one who pays the phone bill gives the other one receipts for payments for the telephone. You can prove long distance calls for business but the IRS will accept only an amount that seems credible for local message units. What seems credible to them may often be less than the truth. How well can you argue? (Bills and checks) [Code Sec. 162]

   b. Answering service, paging service, E-Mail. (Bills and checks) [Code Sec. 162]

12.   Theatrical wardrobe. This is just what it says: a *theatrical* wardrobe, not an ordinary wardrobe item. Conventional street wear is not deductible. The rule says if you *can* wear it on the street, you *can't* deduct it. It doesn't matter if you do in fact wear it in a show. If it isn't nonconventional clothing, you can't have the deduction. The problem with the IRS in Manhattan and Brooklyn is there isn't anything they haven't seen on the street.

There is an exception for musicians, club acts, too, who are required to wear formals. [Fisher, 23 TC 218]

One of my favorite remarks of all time came from a client to whom I had just given the sad news about all the clothes she had bought for her auditions. She said, "My roommate's a model and her accountant takes *her* clothes off." Nice work if you can get it! Knowing someone who got away with it doesn't make something legal.

In TV commercials, they give you a wardrobe allowance. I check W-2 forms for miscellaneous compensation and if wardrobe allowance is indicated, I deduct an equal amount as wardrobe maintenance.

In the N.Y.C. IRS offices, for several years now, many performers have had legwarmers, tights, and leotards disallowed because lots of nondancers buy them to wear as street clothing. Publication 17, page 152 says "(clothing can't be) suitable for ordinary use." What the hell does that mean? A few years ago green surgical tops had a vogue. I wonder if IRS field examiners disallowed any of those when they audited a hospital? I think maybe we should get a law making dance wear a prescription item! To get legwarmers, maybe you should have a note from your choreographer.

Dance wear of all kinds really is nonconventional and should be deductible, but not so so-called rehearsal clothes or audition clothes. Some folks make their own dance clothes—jazz pants, legwarmers, etc. Save receipts for fabrics and notions. (Itemized bills, receipts, checks) [Code Sec. 162; Fisher, 23 TC 218]

13. Wardrobe maintenance. If the wardrobe is deductible, then cleaning it is. (Bills) [Code Sec. 162]

14. Viewing theatre, films, concerts. This is a deduction that the IRS hates. They want you to make an adjustment for personal recreation. I contend that anyone who is in the business is keeping in tune with the dynamics of the profession when attending plays, films, and concerts. The tax courts have ruled that enjoyability is irrelevant to deductibility. However, if you take this deduction and get audited, be prepared to compromise. But don't get piggy! You know what shows have "research" value for you. (Stubs, checks, and diary entries) [Code Sec. 162; Reg. § 1.174-3(a)]

15. Promotional tickets. Only your own ticket is deductible. Not your date's. Unless your date is your agent or a producer or someone like that, in which case deduct their ticket as business promotional expense. (Stubs, checks, and diary entries) [Reg. § 1.162-1; *Blackmer* v. *Com.,* 70 Fed 255]

16. Rehearsal studio rental. (Bills, canceled checks) [Code Sec. 162]

17. Accompanists, arrangers, go-fers, typists, assistants of all types. (Bills and checks) [Code Sec. 162(a)(1)]

18. Office-in-the-home. Prior to January 1, 1976, this was a fairly easy deduction to abuse. Now you can hardly get it at all. The IRS wanted to put an end to the abuses of the deduction by certain professionals who had outside office space and also a little office at home for their own convenience, or people who had salaried jobs and a second part-time business at home and were claiming a big portion of the rent. Section 601 of the Tax Reform Act of 1976 was so strict that it effectively killed the deduction for the majority of show folk. Those of you who work under a union contract that requires that the producer withhold and pay payroll taxes on your behalf are *employees* even if you work only one day. If you are an employee, you must maintain the office in your home for the "convenience of the employer," the producer. There is nothing in most show biz contracts requiring you to keep an office at home. Not understanding that you *must* do your homework to improve and grow in a role and to keep "the mechanism" maintained, Congress has again said, "Tough noogies!" No deduction is allowed for an office in a dwelling unless the following four exceptions and the exclusive and regular use requirements are met:

- Is it your principal place of business?
- Is it used to meet clients, patients, and customers as a matter of course in your business?
- Is it a separate structure used in connection with your business? See "Good News" below.
- Do you store your inventory there?

Obviously, self-employed people don't have to meet the "convenience of the employer" test, but the rest of it applies. If you are self-employed and take a deduction for an office-in-the-home, the IRS wants you to flag your own return by requiring you to answer a question on your return, "Did you claim a deduction for an office in the home?"

GOOD NEWS! In *George H. Weightman, TC Memo 1981-301,* Tax Court has disagreed with the IRS position on the exclusive-use clause! The IRS had disallowed an office set up in a bedroom, claiming that the office was not in a separate room or set off in some physical manner from the rest of the bedroom. The Court observed: "Absent a wall, partition, curtain, or other physical demarcation of the business area, the Court as the trier of fact may well view with a somewhat more critical eye the evidence adduced by the taxpayer to establish that there was, in fact, some separate, though unmarked, space that he used exclusively and on a regular basis as his home office." Since the Internal Revenue Code does not actually use the word "room" in the pertinent section but rather, "a portion of the dwelling unit," the court decided, on the taxpayer's testimony, that a portion of his bedroom was set aside in a relatively formal and definitely distinct arrangement and used exclusively as an office so that he met the exclusive use requirement. He did not get the deduction, however, because the Court also found that this office was not his principal place of business! (He is a teacher.) This is an important case, though, for writers, designers, and artists, if not for performers or musicians unless these last named also teach or coach at home as a *second principal business* or *profession.* Yes, Virginia, you can have more than one principal business! [*Erwin Curphey 1980 73 TC No. 61*] If you can show a business with substantial activity is operated out of your home and that your office furniture is arranged in a separate area, help yourself to the deduction, keeping the limitations of the deduction in mind: You can't deduct an amount greater than the *balance* left after subtracting *all* your other business expenses from your business income. Any leftover deduction can be carried forward to the following year.

A court case I get asked a lot about is *Drucker* v. *Com.,* (1983, CA2) [715 F2d 67, revg TC 605] and *Action on Decision, Ernest Drucker* v. *Com., etc.* Drucker maintained he spent more time rehearsing at home to get ready to rehearse and play with orchestras in auditoriums than he did in the auditoriums. Most musicians and other performers might arguably make the same claim. The Second and Seventh Circuits would agree. The

IRS, however, has not acquiesced in the case, and has instructed itself to take anyone else trying this argument to court. Litigation, anyone?

UPDATE! In January 1990, a court case was reported [Nader Soliman, 94TC No. 3] in which Tax Court considered the use of a home office from the standpoint of the "facts and circumstances" of the case instead of a "focal point" test used in Drucker (home office essential to tax payer's business, he spends substantial time there, and has no other office available).

Employing a facts and circumstances test, Tax Court found that Dr. Soliman could deduct an office-in-the-home despite the fact that all of his income was produced by activities outside the home. Over 30% of his time was spent at home preparing for the other 70% spent working at several different hospitals. Since he had no office at any of the hospitals, the home office was indispensable. Also, since he was incorporated, he was maintaining the office for the convenience of his employer—that is, himself.

An interesting spin-off was the court's decision to let him deduct *all* work-related transportation outside the home! They reasoned since his first trip of the day was on foot down the hall to his home office, every thing else fell outside the first trip/last trip rule (See: Transportation, page 44).

In brief, the "focal point test" of *Drucker* looks only at where the services are performed and where the income is produced. In *Soliman* the court found that the occupation which produces the income requires essential organizational and management activities first and the *place where the management occurs can be the principal place of business.*

Alas and alack! IRS has announced it will not follow *Soliman* and has filed for a reconsideration of the opinion and, furthermore, will appeal if necessary. [IR 90-55, 3/27/90] What does this mean to you? Do you see any parallels with Dr. Soliman's and your modus operandi? If you do and you take a home-office deduction, be prepared to lose it at an audit or take the IRS to Tax Court.

1993 UPDATE: Supreme Court says: IRS 1; Nader Soliman, ZIP! (1/12/93).

In a more recent case [Alfred Hamacher, 94 TC No. 21], an actor-cum-theatre administrator was denied home-office deduction because he claimed justification for both of his "principal businesses" (acting and administrating) while he was given an office at the theatre for his administrative duties. If a person uses one office (at home) to conduct more than one business, each and every one of the business uses must satisfy the requirements or you can't deduct the home office for *any of them.*

There is a curious implication in this matter, however: apparently if Mr. Hamacher had kept his mouth shut on the subject of the administrative work, the Tax Court, applying the "facts and circumstances" test of *Soliman,* would have let him have the home office deduction and all the transportation costs to the theatre. Since it agreed with IRS and disallowed the deduction, out went the baby with the bath water; transportation to the theatre was deemed ordinary commuting and therefore not deductible. Mies was right: "Less is more."

Do you understand all that? Read it again. Tax Court seems to be saying a contract performer, a free-lance, salaried-professional performer can deduct an office in the home. I bet you a dinner at Sabrette's that IRS disagrees. IRS would say that as a performer, the tax-payer is an employee and must maintain the office as a convenience for the theatre. As I read my tax library reporting of the case, Tax Court understands the man to be a "contract actor" whose "home work" is similar to Drucker's and Soliman's *q. v.* This is all well and good, but I don't hold much hope for success for performers because of the exclusive-use clause when considering practice. But if you feel adventuresome, go for it. They only ask for money; they don't shoot you. Yet.

1995 UPDATE: The Contract With America promises to restore more liberal (HAH!) requirements for the home office deduction. Mr. Gingrich, as a visionary of things futuristic, sees the office in the home as the wave of the future. (I wonder what he would think of the idea of making performers, etc. "Statutory Employees"? Would some one or more of his constituents put the question to him??? Please?) Even if the requirements do loosen up, the Treasury will attempt a regulation to squash the deductions of transportation costs to work sites outside the home (See: *Hamacher*, above) because they don't like that.

1998 UPDATE: The new tax act provides that, beginning in 1999, a home office will be your "principle place of business" if you use as your administrative home base and there is no other permanent place where you perform the same duties (such as an office at another location.)

To compute your deduction for office in the home, use Form 8829.

19. Office outside the home. (If you can prove you need one!) (Bills, checks) [Code Sec. 162(a) (3)]
20. Piano tuning, moving, repairs. (Bills, checks) [Code Sec. 212(2)]
21. Repair of equipment used in profession. (Bills and checks) [Code Sec. 212(2); Russell TC Memo 417152, 11 TCM 334]
22. Tax preparation and accounting fees. (Bills and checks) [Pub. 17 (REV. Nov. '87) page 154; Code Sec. 212(3)]
23. Art supplies. (Bills, checks, receipts) [Code Sec. 162]
24. Demo tapes and commercial prints. (Bills and checks) [Reg. § 1.162–1]
25. Trade advertisements. (Bills, checks, and a copy of the ad) [Reg. § 1.162–1]
26. Fabric, notions, scissors sharpening. (Bills, receipts, checks) [Code Sec. 212(2)]

27. Trade papers. (Diary entry, bills, and canceled checks) [Code Sec. 162]
28. Coin phone calls for business. (Diary entry) [Code Sec. 162]
29. Backstage tips. Remember: You can't give gifts to these people. (Checks or diary entry) [Goodrich, O. de H., 20 TC 323]
30. Insurance on instruments or allowable equipment. (Bills, checks) [Code Sec. 212(2)]
31. Copyright fees are part of the expense of producing a work, which expense is treated as equipment (which see!).
32. Equipment used for business. Publication 920 (August 1987) tells us that "the law permits taxpayers to *recover** the cost of property that they use in their employer's trade or business, or that they use to produce income. The cost of property is recovered by depreciating it; that is, taking deductions for the cost over a set period of years." Very nicely put, I'd say; couldn't have put it better, myself! Publication 921 (August 1987) is a good one to latch onto for interesting reading, as is Publication 17, and the instructions that come with Form 4562, which is to be used to report depreciation deductions, and good, old Publication 534, "Depreciation."

      The most recent revision of the law pertaining to depreciation of tangible property (as nice a way of describing equipment as any) is "MACRS."† It applies to all property placed in service after 12/31/86. The property is assigned a designation called a *class*, which can be 3-, 5-, 7-, 10-, 15-, and 20-year property.

      Equipment with an expected useful life of four years or less (and certain race horses!) are 3-year property; four to ten years, 5-year property; ten to sixteen years, 7-year property; and so on. Certain vehicles—computers, office machinery, etc.—are 5-year. Audio and video equipment (other than professional studio equipment) probably is 5-year property. Office furniture and fixtures are 7-year. Musical instruments are as they always have been, mysterious items as to their useful life. This is an area where you're crazy, in my opinion, if'n you don't get a tax preparer. There are many options and restrictions under MACRS, including "expensing"‡ (writing off all—up to $17,500 or your net taxable income—whichever is less—in one year of the cost of equipment) that require some thought and planning on your part. To see if you should expense or depreciate, CWYTP! Incidentally, software cannot be expensed, but must be depreciated. I treat programs cost ing under $100 as small tools. (Bills, receipts, canceled checks, charge slips) [Code Sec. 263 et seq.]

---

*Emphasis added.
†Modified Accelerated Cost Recovery System.
‡Treating an item as a current "expense" rather than a "capital expenditure" to be depreciated.

33. Business entertainment and business gifts. These two deductions are mightily abused by the business world and are, therefore, examined with a keen eye by revenuers. Frankly, I agree with their viewpoint. It's very easy to make a false diary entry for an amount under $75 and claim a business deduction.

Business entertainment is: "sucking-up" expense; polishing the old apple; getting in good with the potentates, the hirers of the wonderful world of show biz. Business entertainment is your *entertaining a potential customer.* What it ain't is your trip to Disney World or that party for sixty people you threw at Fire Island at which most of those present just happened to be theatre types. Wining and dining an agent in an atmosphere conducive to business . . . that's entertainment. A reception held by an agent to introduce the "stable" to a herd of casting directors . . . that's entertainment!

There has to be a reasonable expectation of business resulting from an entertainment expenditure. You see, you're a salesperson. The product you sell is yourself. You can deduct entertainment expenses incurred in selling your product to potential buyers. In your life, who are the buyers? The middlemen? Middlewomen? Hmm? The salesman from Seventh Avenue takes the buyer from Macy's to dinner and a hockey game. *Are you getting the picture?*

Thanks to the efforts of the late Sidney Blackmer and the wisdom of the Court of Appeals [*Blackmer* v. *Com.,* Acq.], show folk have somewhat less-strict requirements for deducting entertainment expense in regard to circumstances, requirement by an employer, direct conduct of business (as opposed to related conduct of business). The court observed (approximately) that actors and others in the performing professions are frequently known to entertain to keep up their public image, the demand for their services, and so forth. This doesn't mean you can play Good Time Charlie at a bar and write it off! You have to demonstrate the business purpose of the expense, but you don't have to "make a sale" on the spot, and the expense doesn't have to be required by your employer. The court seems to have recognized that in show biz, one doesn't have one employer; that show folk operate like independent contractors (in spite of the technicality of withholding when working under a union contract); that getting employed is "making a sale"; that goods and money don't change hands in the Biz, services and money do, talent and money do.

The underlying principles of business entertainment hold that it must be ordinary and necessary to the conduct of business. Making yourself desirable and attractive to a producer or director or agent is how you push your product; it's part of making a sale.

The Treasury says you can entertain people with whom you could reasonably expect to do business. Purely social occasions are not deductible, and partly social occasions must be apportioned. Actors can entertain anyone who could hire them or help them get hired; directors, producers, writers, designers can entertain the same gang of bandits plus professional advisers, employees, "customers," "suppliers," etc. Ask yourself again, "Who are the buyers?" Who in your work experience fit these definitions?

How much is deductible? If all other requirements are met, deduct 50 percent of amounts "deemed not lavish or extravagant *under the circumstances*". Don't make the 50% computation unless you are using Schedule C-EZ. Form 2106 or Schedule C makes it for you. So put down 100% on those forms. Show business entertaining usually takes the form of wining and dining and/or buying tickets for your show for show business potentates. (If you, gentle reader, are not in show biz, who are the potentates in your racket?) You can put on the feedbag at home or in a restaurant, but when you entertain at home, you must make an apportionment for your own ribs and juice. Only the *extra* cost of food and booze because of the presence of business associates is deductible, and they must be present for business, not just incidentally or socially.

What do you need to substantiate entertainment expense? If the cost is $75 or more, you absolutely must have receipts. For any amount, you must have copious diary notations that give sufficient detail explaining: *who* it was, what the *person's title* is, *company's name,* what you *discussed.* What *business* was *conducted.*

Once again, that's *name, title, company, business discussed.* Your receipts and diary entries must "complement each other in an orderly fashion" and be complete. "Lunch with Zelda" won't do. Here are some good examples of diary notations: "Dinner at Sardi's with Bill Bogert, Agent, Famous Pains Agency. Discussed his representing me." "Staff of CBS casting dept. to meet my clients (list them) at office from 4:00 to 6:00." "Two tix for Joe Pep, Producer/Director, Garter

Falls Little Theatre." Are you getting it? Spell it out! Don't be cryptic!

Charge restaurant bills whenever possible. Get receipts from liquor stores. The IRS is understandably skeptical of checks to liquor stores and supermarkets since these establishments frequently allow customers to cash checks. But do save canceled checks, in addition to receipts. When buying tix for agents and others to see you perform, ask those nice box-office folks to oblige you with a receipt stating, for example, "2 tix for *George M* for Joe Pep paid by Ima Starr."

The rules state these diary notations must be made contemporaneously with the expense . . . not two years later on the night before your audit. Get in the habit of doing it right away.

Those of you who are likely to be having a deductible reception, get a guest book and ask everyone to "sign in, please!"

Do not lump gifts and entertainment together on your return! You lose 50% of entertainment, but ya don't have to lose anything from gifts. Speaking of which . . .

The same people who can be entertained can be given deductible gifts . . . with a $25 per person, per year, limitation. Diary entries are no good for gifts. You must have a receipt, and it must be notated: *name, title, company.* Viz: "Gift for India Temple, Production Manager, SuperAte Films." Opening night presents for fellow cast members are *not deductible.*

One last word on this subject: Don't give dressers, doormen, or crew members gifts. They are not deductible. Give them money. By check. (See paragraph 29, "Backstage tips," above.) (Charge slips, paid bills, receipts, diary) [*Blackmer* v. *Com.* 70 F2d 255; Code Sec. 274 et seq]

34. Transportation and travel expenses. Sooner or later, every performing artist works out-of-town and every writer, director, producer, and so on travels for casting or research. Traveling is expensive and, in the case of performers, frequently audited.

    The first thing the IRS wants to know at an audit is if you were indeed traveling for your employer; then, were you reimbursed for living expenses on the road. So, save your contracts and attached riders. If you misplace a contract, you can always get a duplicate from your union. Some contracts do entail some reimbursement. You should learn which ones do and keep some sort of account of how much per diem you have received. Save the paycheck stubs which show per diem. Your contract will prove some or all of these facts:

- You were working
- Where you were working (maybe)
- The starting date of the job
- The contemplated closing date (maybe)
- Your salary
- Per diem (maybe)
- Extras (rooms provided, for example)
- Special riders (billing, favored nations, etc.)

It is important to keep any itineraries you may be provided with. They'll help supply a lot of information at an audit and help expedite getting your case closed.

Here's a checklist of deductions for which the Treasury regulations accept a properly kept diary as adequate evidence if you are claiming actual cost of expenses. (See Appendix III and *use* it!)

Meals: A daily *aggregate* amount is acceptable.*

Laundry/Dry Cleaning: Save receipts for dry cleaning and finish work— pressing of shirts, slacks, and so on. Enter those amounts in addition to laundromats used in the diary.

Local Transportation While on the Road: Commuting to work is not deductible *at home,* but it is when you're away from home with a show. Buses and cabs, from where you're lodging to where you're eating and to the theatre and back are deductible and go in the diary.

Local Transportation in Your Home City: The exceptions being noted, the rule is that you cannot deduct commuting to work. However, self-employeds work at home, so outside business errands are deductible. Employees can deduct any unreimbursed errand running. Sometimes it is understood that a stage manager, for example, will do some errand running and not be reimbursed. Going from one job location to another in the same day, from a rehearsal to a fitting and back to rehearsal are some examples of local transportation "at home" that are deductible. When working in more than one location in the same day, the first trip out and last trip home are not deductible.

Tips: Tipping porters, chambermaids, dressers, stagedoormen, etc.

Coin phone calls to your union, agent, answering service, or anyone else related to your business.

*Publication 463, pages 12–14, 1987

Remember: Any item over $75 *must be receipted.* A diary entry alone is *not* acceptable.

Starting with 1993 returns, you can no longer deduct expenses if the job lasts more than a year at a distant site, even if the job began in 1992. Equity is working on it.

Here's a checklist of deductions that must be receipted, no matter what the amount, if you claim actual expenses.

Lodging: Review what makes a good paid itemized bill and begin checking your hotel bills against that standard. Many hotel bills fail the test. Insist on all the proper information on your bill. Be especially careful about bills from rooming and boarding houses in smaller towns and summer stock country.

Auto rental: If you're playing a town like Los Angeles, where public transportation is sketchy or nonexistent, and you rent a car to get back and forth from the theatre, you can deduct it. So save the receipt. If you're sharing the car, let the person who actually rents it make nice receipts for the others, spelling out what it was for, the cost to each one, signed and dated. Also save gas receipts for rented cars, tolls, and parking.

Transportation: Any time you return home from the road at your own expense for business (auditions, interviews) you can deduct it. If the trip is just for a change or any personal reason, it is deductible up to an amount equal to what you've been paying for meals and lodging on the road. I know a guy who always checks out the callboard at Equity and visits his agent whenever he returns to New York from the road on a day off. This eases his conscience and he deducts every penny of the fare. Always use a charge card for fares, if you can, so if you lose the ticket, you'll have another substantiation. No tickee, no deductee!

Transportation to a temporary job daily beyond the general area of your "tax home" is deductible if you return home each night (another exception to the rule that says you cannot deduct commuting to work). *Example:* You live in New York and get a show at Papermill Playhouse in Millburn, New Jersey. It's temporary and beyond the general area of your "tax home" and you return to New York each night. You take the train or a bunch of you rent a car. It's deductible.

UPDATE: Time to celebrate! Rev Rul 90-23, 1990-11 IRB states a somewhat changed position on daily, local transportation to job sites: you still can't deduct local transportation costs to one or more *regular* places of business, but if you have one or more regular places of business you can deduct commuting to and from your home and a *temporary* job site within your tax home locality.

To illustrate: a regular on a soap opera who gets a commercial can deduct the cost of going to and from that shoot. Another example: you work at a scenic studio in the Bronx and the boss says to you, "Walter, for the next six days I want you to go into Manhattan and work with the designer and production stage manager, Frank, at the Kilfenora Theatre." The cost of commuting between midtown and Walter and Margaret's little blue heaven is deductible now. Neat, huh?

Fares While Looking for Work: A 1975 revenue ruling allowed expenses looking for work in your regular profession to be deducted from gross income. (Write amounts for public street transportation in your diary, or if making rounds in your own car, write the mileage in your appointment book or tax expense book.)

For major intercity fares, *save the tickets.*

If you go to the coast (either one!) for an extended time and the *majority* of that time is spent making rounds, you can deduct all the living expenses, just as if you were there working. The regular record-keeping requirements for travel apply. I suggest you keep copious notes of every appointment and call to make appointments on these junkets as the IRS is rightly suspicious of oral testimony regarding these expenses. "I was checking out the scene in L.A." won't get you through an audit. Travel as a form of education is no longer allowed.

Telephone: Annotate business calls on your hotel bills. If you are at a regional, dinner, or stock theatre and have a phone installed during your stay, check off business calls on the bill. If you use someone else's phone, get the charges from the operator and have your friend make you a bill.

Utilities: If you're in the provinces for an extended stint and rent an apartment and have to pay gas and electric, it's deductible.

Under some Equity and SAG contracts you get a per diem allowance to pay for expenses. The Equity Production Contract, for example, pays a flat weekly (pro-rated for partial weeks) and in most cases it is less than the per diem federal employees get. This last fact is what keeps the per diem from showing up on the W-2 form as "other compensation." When an Equity tour plays a small enough town, the Equity per diem allowance may be more than the federal per diem rate. When this happens, the excess per diem times the number of days it is paid shows up on the W-2 form with the letter L in front of it in box 17 and is taxable to you. There are various options available to you for dealing with the per diem:

1. If you spent as much as or less than the per diem and it hasn't been reported either entirely or in part, you can ignore the whole topic on your tax return. It's a wash.
2. If you spent more than the per diem, you can claim your expenses and account for the per diem (subtract it), the difference becoming a deduction to you. You will need to: 1) prove your expenses by showing evidence of actual cost, or 2) claim the

High/Low Optional Federal Per Diem Rates or CONUS (Continental U.S.) Per Diem Rates (these rates are sometimes more and sometimes less than the high/low option), *whichever is less,* #1 or #2. A curious loophole seems to present itself here: unless you have saved proof of actual cost under the record keeping requirements outlined above, how can you prove that you didn't spend less than the high/low optional rates or CONUS rates? Will you ever be required to prove that you didn't do something? Stranger things have happened!

Incidentally, you cannot mix and match the two federal per diem rates to get the highest deduction; you must use one or the other consistently for the year.

3. If you spent less than the per diem and it has been reported, the difference is negative and reduces the amount of the rest of your deductions. In other words, you wind up paying some tax on some of the per diem—whatever you can't account for. This most frequently happens with SAG per diem, because they pay for the hotel, schlep you around, give you breakfast and lunch, and sometimes dinner. Sometimes California companies report the per diem as "living expense" on a California 1099 and withhold state taxes. The state taxes are deductible on your federal Schedule A—small comfort—but California will be looking for a return from you. Now given the fact that there was practically nothing to spend the per diem on under the circumstances, you're gonna owe!! Oh, well, it's all part of life's rich tapestry.

As far as I can tell, all theatrical and film employers are assuming that the per diem arrangements with the unions are "accountable plans." That's IRSese for: "the employee has accounted to the employer in an IRS-satisfactory way, thereby relieving the employer from reporting the per diem on the W-2 Forms and the employee from dealing with it on his or her tax return." A per diem arrangement qualifies as "an accountable plan" if the employee 1) proves the proper use of the per diem to the employer, 2) there is a business connection to the arrangement, and 3) the employee is required to return the unspent per diem to the employer.

The first condition is met *de facto* when the per diem is equal to or less than those federal per diem rates. (That's the Equity per diem all over). The second condition seems to explain itself. As far as I know no producer is requiring Equity members to return unspent per diems at the end of the week or the run. It would seem then that the arrangement is not an accountable plan and the per diem should be on the W-2 Form. But what do I know?

Under an accountable plan I assume they are saying that you have sub-
stantiated to the Fed's satisfaction any amounts up to the federal employee
per diems and no questions asked, thank you very much. If the employer
pays your hotel bill (as in SAG jobs) the per diem considered proved is only
the amount for meals and incidental expenses (M&IE) and if that's $75 or
$100 a day, you're in deep doo-doo if the SAG per diem is reported and you
don't have proof of actual cost. And in all but foreign locales, that SAG per
diem will be more than the M&IE rate.

The rates and locations are adjusted every year. For 1997, the rates for
the optional High/Low substantiation method for MIE in the continental
U.S. are:

High = $40/day
Low = $32/day

Beginning on the next page is a swell list of the High Cost cities and
locales. Notice that some of them are seasonal.

The CONUS Rate options are town specific and the list goes on for
page after page. Hundreds of towns are on the list. Sometimes CONUS rates
are higher, sometimes lower. However, you can't combine both rates to get
the higher; you have to use one method or the other for the year. Where can
you get the CONUS tables? Try your local IRS public information office.
Try calling *Tax-payers' Assistance*. Get your local number from the Blue
Pages—the government listings in your phone book. Read that whole thing
again two or three times.

For foreign travel, there are similar established rates of per diems. A
government publication issued monthly to adjust the frequently changing
cost of travel, etc. in foreign locales has the imposing title: *Maximum Travel
Per Diem Allowances for Foreign Areas, Section 925, a Supplement to the
Standard Regulations (Government Civilians, Foreign Areas).* Try an IRS
library or Tax-payers' Assistance. This supplement usually includes a bul-
letin with the rates for the non-foreign localities outside the "lower 48."

Self-employed persons report travel expense on a detailed statement
attached to Schedule C.

Employees report their business expenses on Form 2106. If you go on
the road more than once or for more than one employer, Form 2106 doesn't
allow you to go into much detail. The more information you can supply with
the return, the less you may have to supply at an audit, so consider attaching
a detailed schedule to Form 2106. Your expenses in excess of amount of
reimbursement will wind up on Schedule A as a "miscellaneous" deduction.
Qualified Performing Artists (QPA) go directly to Form 1040 from 2106 and
NOT Sched. A.

A special word on convention and/or foreign travel is in order. The

Locations Eligible for Optional High Cost, Standard Meal Allowance
(Locations Not Listed are Eligible for Low Cost Rate)

City	Locale or County
Arizona	
Grand Canyon	Grand Canyon National Park, Kaibab National Forest, and all points in Coconino County
Phoenix/Scottsdale (Oct. 1–May 14)	Maricopa
California	
Gualala/Point Arena	Medocino
Los Angeles	Los Angeles, Kern, Orange, and Ventura Counties; Edwards Air Force Base; Naval Weapons Center and Ordnance Test Station, China Lake
Palo Alto/San Jose	Santa Clara
San Francisco	San Francisco
South Lake Tahoe	El Dorado
Yoesmite Nat'l Park (April 1–Oct. 31)	Mariposa
Colorado	
Aspen (Jan. 15–Mar. 31)	Pitkin
Keystone/Silverthorne	Summit
Steamboat Springs (Dec. 1–Mar. 31)	Routt
Telluride	San Miquel
Vail (Nov. 1–Mar. 31)	Eagle
District of Columbia	
Washington, D.C.	Washington, D.C.; the cities of Alexandria, Falls Church and Fairfax, and the counties of Arlington, Loudoun, and Fairfax in Virginia; and the counties of Montgomery and Prince Georges in Maryland
Florida	
Key West	Monroe
Illinois	
Chicago	Du Page, Cook, and Lake
Maine	
Bar Harbor (July 1–Sept. 14)	Hancock
Maryland	
Ocean City (May 1–Sept. 30)	Worcester
Saint Michaels	Talbot

City	Locale or County
Massachusetts	
Boston	Suffolk
Cambridge/Lowell	Middlesex
Hyannis	Barnstable
(July 1–Sept. 30)	
Martha's Vineyard/	
Nantucket	Dukes and Nantucket
Michigan	
Leland	Leelanau
(May 1–Sept. 30)	
Mackinac Island	Mackinac
(June 1–Sept. 30)	
Nevada	
Incline Village	Incline Village
Stateline	Douglas
New Jersey	
Atlantic City	Atlantic
(Apr. 1–Nov. 30)	
Ocean City/Cape May	Cape May
(May 15–Sept. 30)	
New Mexico	
Santa Fe	Santa Fe
(May 1–Oct. 31)	
New York	
New York City	The boroughs of Bronx, Brooklyn, Manhattan, Queens, and Staten Island
Long Island	Nassau and Suffolk
White Plains	Westchester
North Carolina	
Duck/Outer Banks	Dare
(May 1–Sept. 30)	
Ohio	
Sandusky	Erie
(May 1–Sept. 30)	
Pennsylvania	
Chester/Radnor	Delaware
Philadelphia	Philadelphia
Bala Cynwyd	Montgomery County
Rhode Island	
Newport/Block Island	Newport and Washington
(May 1–Oct. 14)	

City	Locale or County
Tennessee	
Nashville	Brown
(Jun. 1–Oct. 31)	
Utah	
Bullfrog	Garfield
(April 1–Oct. 31)	
Park City	Summit
(Dec. 1–Mar. 31)	
Virginia	
Virginia Beach	Virginia Beach, Norfolk, Portsmouth
(May 1–Sept. 30)	and Chesapeake
Wintergreen	Nelson
Wyoming	
Jackson	Teton
(June 1–Oct. 14)	

same record-keeping rules apply, of course, but you can save yourself a lot of grief if you remember a couple of facts:

1. Your receipts probably aren't in English.
2. You didn't pay in dollars.

Make notes of exchange rates. You probably won't remember them and approximations won't serve. Make currency conversions on bills and also annotate what the items are while you still know. If you charge meals or laundry to your hotel bill in Paris and neither you nor your tax person speaks French, how are you going to itemize your expenses? And if you're audited, don't expect to get a multilingual examiner.

Attention, directors, producers, writers, designers, journalists, and others who attend foreign conventions: you can deduct only two per year! And that isn't the worst! Transportation is limited to the lowest economy or coach fare no matter what "class" you actually fly!

If at least 50 percent of the days away—including travel days—aren't spent in business-related activities, you must prorate expenses using a fraction of business days over total days away. Living expenses are limited to the per diem rate given government employees serving in the same area as the convention. To qualify as a business day, there must be at least six hours of activities scheduled that day and you must attend and be able to prove you attended two-thirds of the activities that day. If only three hours of activities are scheduled and you attend at least two of them, you can deduct half a day's subsistence. If you attend two-thirds of all the activities scheduled for the whole convention, you needn't worry about the two-thirds on a particular day.

To claim the convention expenses, you have to attach to your return a statement signed by an officer of the convention attesting that you complied with the requirements for deducting foreign convention expenses (a note from mother!). You must also attach a statement showing the dates of the trip and the convention, the number of hours devoted to convention activities, a program of all the convention activities, and a brochure describing the convention.

All this should make you carefully consider which conventions to attend if you have a choice of more than two in one year and think twice about combining a convention with a vacation.

A fundamental point: travel expenses are deductible only if you maintain a permanent residence somewhere. This location is called your "tax home." Your tax home is the place where you principally reside, where you vote and go to church or temple, where your family or friends are, and the place that is your *principal place of business.* The most important factors in deciding what is your tax home are where you reside and where you obtain your work. You must incur substantial expense at that place to claim it as home. The travel expenses will be deductible if you have *double residence* expense. To wit, let me tell you the sad story of the actor who got a part in a national company, *sublet* his apartment, claimed travel expenses on his tax return, got audited by the IRS, couldn't show proof of rent paid on his New York apartment because the sublet paid the landlord, lost the expenses deduction, and had to pay back $1,850 in taxes. Use your head!

NOTE: You cannot deduct travel and transportation if any job takes you away from home for more than a year, even if the period falls over two or three tax years. If the IRS catches on that you've been out with *Phantom,* for example, for 20 months, you lose your tax home and, I presume, owe income tax on all that per diem. What to do, what to do? Oh, musha-mush ochone! Then there are state and city taxes! Veh ist mir! Then penalty and interest! Could any thing be worse?

Needless to say, there are other deductions that fall into the miscellaneous category. Unless there is an exception in law or ruling, anything you buy to help you earn money is deductible to the extent it is not reimbursed by your employer. If you have any doubt as to whether any purchase is deductible, save admissible evidence anyway and CWYTP!

Other Miscellaneous Deductions

1. Federal estate tax on income in respect of a decedent.
2. Amortizable bond premium.
3. Gambling losses to the extent of gambling winnings.
4. Unrecovered investment in pension.

Am I ringing any bells?

5. Repayments under claim of right.
6. Impairment-related work expenses. If you are handicapped, you can deduct expenses of work if they are impairment related. (Bills, canceled checks) [Publication 17, page 154]

Tax Credits

After you have reached the point on your return where you calculate your tax obligation by one of several methods, you have available to you "Tax Credits." Tax Credits are:

- Credit for child and dependent care expenses
- Credit for the elderly or for the permanently and totally disabled
- Foreign tax credit
- General business credit
- Earned income credit (EIC)

Child and Dependent Care Expenses

If you maintain a household (pay for more than 50 percent of the upkeep) and a dependent child—twelve years old or younger—is living with you, or a dependent adult who is incapable of caring for himself, or a spouse who is incapable of caring for himself, you may take a percentage of the cost of *employment-related* expenditures for the care of this qualified individual in your absence. There is a dollar limitation to the amount of the credit: up to a **percentage of a maximum of** $2400 for one qualifying individual or $4800 for two or more qualifying individuals. The percentage of expenses allowable is based on **AGI** and runs from 30% for AGIs not exceeding $10,000 to 20% for AGIs of $28,000 and up. Also the amount of the credit cannot exceed the income you earn. In the case of a married couple, it cannot exceed the lesser amount earned by either spouse.

Employment-related expenses are those expenses, such as baby-sitters or day-care centers, which enable you or your spouse to be gainfully employed or to seek gainful employment. Of course, you must prorate payments if the time put in by the sitter, for example, includes any nonemployment related time. To illustrate: You and your spouse both work and normally arrive home at 6:00 P.M., at which time the sitter leaves. One night you decide to meet after work and go to dinner and a show. The time after 6:00 is not employment-related and cannot be included when calculating the credit. Get Publication 503 for more details.

Care outside the home is deductible only for a dependent child under fourteen years of age or another qualifying person who spends at least eight hours per day in your household. In the home, care is deductible for all qualified individuals.

The care, to be deductible, has to be for the welfare, the well-being of the qualified individual. Payments to a gardener, for example, couldn't be deducted. There are many restrictions. CWYTP!

You can deduct payments to a relative for child and dependent care, as long as that relative is not a dependent of yours and the service performed by that relative qualifies as employment as defined by the Social Security Act. If you leave your child at the home of a relative, payments may not be deductible since you may not have control—an employer's control—over the situation. You'd have to establish that you do have control over the situation and that an employer-employee relationship does pertain.

You must withhold, match, and file FICA tax for any individuals you pay for dependent care in your home. Get help from your local IRS office or your tax person.

You must keep the following records for this credit:

- Itemized statements from the sitter.
- Proof of payment of the sitter's fees.
- If you use a day-care center, save their bills and your canceled checks.

Credit for the Elderly or for the Permanently and Totally Disabled

If you are over sixty-five or under sixty-five, and permanently and totally disabled when you retired, did not reach mandatory retirement age before 1987 and you received taxable disability benefits, and are a U.S. citizen or resident, you may claim this credit. There are limitations on AGI, amount of nontaxable social security or other pension income, disability income.

Publication 17 and the instructions for Schedule R set forth these limitations and describe the computation. If you fall within the qualifications described above, it is worth getting either Publication 17 or Schedule R instructions to see if you can get the credit.

Other Credits

Here are the other credits available to individuals. They are not of general interest, but if any apply to you, CWYTP or get the appropriate publication, form, and/or instructions from the IRS. Some of the forms are:

- Mortgage Interest Credit (Form 8396)
- Investment Credit (Form 3468)
- Jobs Credit (Form 5884)
- Low-Income Housing Credit (Form 8586)

NEW FOR 1998

Child Tax Credit. For each qualified child (dependent under 17) $400. ($500 starting in '99)

HOPE Scholarship Credit. During the first two years of your child's college, you can take a credit of up to 100% of the first $1000 per student, per year, and 50% of the next $1000 you spend on your own or your spouse or dependent for a maximum of $1500.

Lifetime learning credit. You can elect to take a 20% credit of up to $5000 of education expense—graduate or undergraduate—paid after June 30, 1998. You can take the credit for more than two years.

NOTE: You should use whichever of the two credits gives you the best tax break. There are "phase-out" income levels. You can't claim the credit if you file Married-filing-separately.

Qualified electric vehicle credit (Form 8834)

Qualified adoption expenses (Form 8839)

Earned Income Credit

All of the tax credits discussed or mentioned heretofore can reduce your tax liability to zero dollars but not more than that. You can recover all your withholding and/or estimated tax payments but you can't get back more than was withheld using those there credits. Mais, mes amis, there is another credit—the Earned Income Credit! C'est vrai! Want to hear about it? Read on, Macheath!

To get the Earned Income Credit you must meet these "eligibility requirements":

1. *You must have* a qualifying child—that is, a child who . . .
   is your son or daughter . . . or . . .
   a descendant of either . . . . . . no *good if that* child is married
            by the end of the taxable year
                        . . . *but it's ok if* . . . *you* are en
                        titled to a dependency exemption for that
                        child under Code Section 151 or would
                        have been entitled to that deduction *except* for
                        a divorce agreement relinquishing it
                        under code Sec.152(e)(2), etc. etc. CWYTP! . . . *or* . . .

a legally adopted child . . . *or* . . .
a child placed with you by an agency for legal adoption. . . *or*. . .
a stepson or stepdaughter . . . or . . .
an eligible foster child who is someone you take care of
   as you would your own child and who lives with you
   for the whole tax year . . . *and* . . .
if it's your child, the child must live with you in the US
   for more than half the year but a foster child must live
   with you for the whole year . . . *and* . . .
the child has not reached his/her 19th year during your tax year . . . *but it's
   ok* . . .
if the child is a full-time student who has not reached the
   age 24 during the year . . . *but* . . .
the individual is considered to have met the age restrictions
   if totally and permanently disabled during the tax
   year. That's doing it the hard way!
                                    or
2. You *can* be childless by the qualifications above but be the person
   qualifying for the EIC (acronym alert!!) if your principal
   place of residence has been the US for more than half the year
   . . . *and* . . .
            you were older than 24 but less than 65 before the year's
                        end . . . *and* . . .
            you're not anyone else's dependent for tax purposes
                        . . . *or* . . .
            you're not a nonresident alien . . . or. . .
            you're not someone else's "qualifying child" . . . *or* . . .
            you haven't claimed foreign income or foreign housing
                        exclusion . . . *and* . . .
            if married, you file a joint return . . . *unless* . . .
            you're a married person living apart from your spouse at
                        least for the last six months of the year and maintaining
                        an abode for yourself and a child and qualify to file

separately or singly under the "abandoned spouse" rule, –q.v. or CWYTP!

So, all this means you are qualified, or not, to have money over and above or in addition to your withholding and estimated tax payments applied to your tax liability, and whatever is in excess of your tax liability sent to you in a check as part of a refund of overpayment. I would say "you'd get it *back*" except you never had the EIC money to begin with but let's not quibble over semantics.

How much you get depends on a table which sets rates and percentages depending on whether you have no qualifying children or one or two, what your *earned income* amounts to, and what your AGI is. The credit is indexed for inflation and changes every year. Schedule EIC is the one to use. There are EIC Tables and worksheets in the 1040 Instructions to compute the credit and some calculations are required. The worksheet actually isn't too bad as IRS worksheets go, but keep John Jameson handy for consultation and communion services.

IRS will figure the credit for you if you file Form 1040, enter on the appropriate line (near the end of the form) any advanced EIC payments you may have received from your employer, fill in the information requested on Schedule EIC if you have a qualifying child, and write *"EIC"* next to the appropriate line (somewhere in the 50's lines).

1040EZ, 1040A have their own instructions for getting IRS to do it for you and, indeed, doing it for yourself. But I hope you are lucky enough to be doing the long form and getting all those unfortunate deductions we have been learning about along the way.

The requirements and the benefits of the EIC have changed every year so don't expect anything you've read to remain unchanged. Especially since the 1995 Congress has been snorting and pawing the ground, posturing, blathering, and poking holes in the air with their fingers. If I were a vulgar person, I would call them the biggest bunch of cold-hearted, unchristian, arse-licking, selfish, hypocritical, pandering sons-of-bitches to come down the pike in the long history of pikes. They call themselves Christians and they're in bed with the Christian Right, but I wonder how many of them have ever read the Gospels? Don't get me started! Just remember what Mr. Twain said: "It could probably be shown by facts and figures that there is no distinctively native American criminal class, except Congress." Their only principles are the ones they used to get elected or re-elected claiming to obey the will of the people. Well, sometimes the will of the people is ungenerous at best and disgraceful when it gets a full head of steam. What has this to do with EIC? Just this: don't count on it to remain on the books.

6

Audit Examinations

If you keep the kind of records I've been suggesting you keep, an audit examination doesn't have to be any more painful than having your throat ripped out by a casting director. But seriously, folks, aside from the unpredictable disposition of the examiner, who may or may not hate what you do for a living, an examination is the IRS saying, "Come on down! It's Show and Tell time!" Those hard-working folks at the IRS just want to look at all that stuff crammed into the Capezio shoe box in the bottom of your closet.

You Get Cast

As an individual taxpayer, you get an invitation to appear at your local IRS office and "please be prepared to substantiate the following items." They give you a date and a time, and a number to call if you can't keep the appointment.

If you ignore them, they don't go away. If you ignore this first little billet-doux, the computer will send you a second letter, the so-called "30-day letter." It's a report of findings saying that, based on the information you provided (which was no information at all), (something like) "We have disallowed all your deductions and you owe us (so much) and if you want to do something about it, please contact us within thirty days, thank you very much."

If you ignore this one, the "90-day letter" comes! This one must be attended to. A clock is running. You have to do something within the 90-day period or pay the tax. But even if you pay the tax, you can still file a "Claim for Refund," giving your sad tale why you didn't do something to comply with the request to show your records ("My roommate wasn't forwarding my mail!), and maybe they'll reopen the case and examine your records.

Why Me?

If you're wondering why thespians and others in the Biz get audited so much, let me explain. A set of standards, or norms, for expenses and de-

ductions are arrived at through a system of random-selection audits—
TCMP audits (Taxpayer Compliance Measurement Program)—every three
years. The results of these audits supposedly tell the IRS what are normal
amounts of deductions in several income brackets. Exactly how they use
this information is largely kept secret. *UPDATE:* IRS announced on
10/23/95 indefinite postponement of TCMP audits.

Anyway, let's say you fall in the same income bracket as a Union bus
driver one year. Your return is scored by the Discriminant Function of the
computer the same as the bus driver's. You might get audited while he does-
n't because the average "bear" doesn't spend all that money, all that elu-
sive "green," the multitudes of "spondulicks" that a freelance professional
does. His deductions aren't anywhere near what yours are, because you have
all those on-going expenses year in and year out. Until the IRS starts to fac-
tor what you do for a living into the computer's program, and gets some
audit history for each occupation, they'll never be able to handicap and you
and yours will continue to get audited a lot. What are you going to do? Grin
and bear it. It goes with the territory.

Rehearsal

If you get an audit letter, get out that shoe box, get your stuff out and start
to sort it out. Check the audit letter to see *what* it is they want to examine.
If it says "medical," sort all your medical expenses into a pile. If it says
"travel and entertainment" or "employee business expenses" (which you call
road expense) get that stuff sorted out.

DON'T TAKE what they haven't asked for! You'll just clutter up the
examiner's desk and get yourself nervous. It'll get in your way and his, so
put it away. Simplicity and neatness here will help.

Next, taking one category at a time, and referring to your return,
arrange the items within the category in the order in which they appear on
the return. When each category is sorted out and arranged, put the stuff
into separate envelopes, put a rubber band around it, do something to keep
them from getting mixed up with something else. The purpose of all this
neatness is so that when the examiner says, "Let's see 'medical,' " you re-
spond promptly with the right stuff. His job is to get you examined, the case
closed, and you out of there. This is so he'll look good to his supervisor,
and get promoted, and become commissioner some day. He has a work load
he's expected to keep up with, and any little detailed thing you can do to
further his getting that work done quickly will stand *you* in good stead. If
you help him by being prepared, he's got to be better disposed toward you
than those fools who dump everything on his desk in a jumble.

Why would you want to anger someone who has his hand in your
pocket? It doesn't make sense. Do the best you can to help the person do
the job. Most of the examiners I have known are decent, competent folks.

They didn't pick your return for audit. *Most* of them have no bones to pick, nor do they assume you've done anything wrong. (Whenever the IRS thinks you've done something wrong, they *investigate* you and you don't know it until they get the goods on you.) Local office examiners are just looking for errors. And inadvertent errors at that. Advertent errors are handled by another department.

Opening

An audit typically opens with a trio of standard questions to which you give truthful answers: "Have you filed all prior returns?"; "Have you declared all of your income?"; "Did you have any barter income?"

Let's say you're being examined on your travel expense. Show your contract, point out any riders, and point out per diem on the W-2, if any. The examiner will then get into the expenses themselves and will ask to see hotel receipts, plane tickets, auto rental receipts, your diary, and so on, and at the end may ask for additional information or some verification from your employer. You, of course, will be more than happy to get any letters or additional substantiation requested.

During the proceedings, he may ask you to explain the business nature of a deduction or to read something from your diary. He may ask something like, "What are 'pix'?"; "Why do you need an answering service?" So, tell him! He or she may not know much about show biz, but on the other hand, you probably know squat about tax biz!

During the audit, don't let the long silences get to you. Sometimes deadly minutes go by while an examiner pores over some bill or other and your mouth begins to think it needs to run. Bring a good book to the audit. Write "Shut up!" at the top of every page.

Playing Your Role

Strategy is very important. I've already explained that getting organized is going to benefit you by making the examiner's job easier, so *get organized!* Bring paper and pencil to make notes. Be as pleasant as you can under circumstances that are sure to make the body shaky. Don't let the examiner put words in your mouth. If he suggests that you have spent rather lavishly in restaurants entertaining, for goodness' sake disagree, and then explain all the business benefit you either have or hope to derive from this entertaining: *It's an investment in yourself.* It's a marketplace out there and you're in it and you have to do what any salesperson does. You gotta know the territory!

If your income in the year being audited was low, go to the audit prepared to show how you survived, what nontaxable sources of income you may have had: You're being kept; you had a Federal refund from the year before; you withdrew money from savings, Daddy helped, whatever.

Hecklers

Try to remain composed if you've drawn an idiot for an examiner. IRS personnel are protected by law from verbal abuse. On the other hand, you don't have to, as my brother Robert puts it, "take any crap from anyone." You don't have to suffer someone completely ignorant of what you do for a living, or demonstrably prejudiced, or with whom you're having a bad personality clash. Respectfully request to see the supervisor and ask for a better shake. There was once an examiner in the Manhattan office who told me that "actors get audited a lot because we know they cheat a lot on their returns." We finished that conversation in his supervisor's office. IRS examiners are supposed to be trained to apply the law fairly and reasonably; they should not "get an attitude" and begin interpreting the law in a narrow fashion with an eye to collecting revenue, or teaching a lesson to any particular group of taxpayers—not even rogues, vagabonds, or buskers. If you think you're getting an unreasonable examination, start taking notes. Ask for a basis, a reason, a citation for every disallowance, because if you want to appeal an adverse determination, you want to be able to quote the reasons you were given.

A word, please, about "policy." I have encountered many examiners in Manhattan who say, "Our *policy* is to allow only half the makeup claimed by females" or "Our policy is to allow only half of theatre tickets." The last time I looked, Congress was making the policies. Tax Court was making the policies. Circuit Court, District Court, and Supreme Court were making the policies. It's difficult to say what to do. You save receipts for what is used for business, and they want to disallow some for personal use! What to do? I say stick to your guns! Tell them that you don't save receipts for personal makeup or shows which have no possibilities for you. Be prepared to compromise.

The Reviews Are In

When all items have been covered, one of three determinations is made:

1. "No change." This means your return has been accepted as filed. Contain your excitement until you've left the building. After a few weeks you'll get a form letter informing you officially of the determination. SAVE THIS LETTER! The IRS has a program to avoid repeat audits. If you get an audit no-

    tice after being audited on the same items and owed little or no tax, they'd like to let you out of the audit. If you've saved the paper work on the prior audit, that will facilitate canceling the next.

2. "Change/no change." This indicates some adjustments but the resulting tax was less than $50, so they're not bothering to collect.

3. "A change." One of two changes is possible: They owe you or you owe them. When there are disallowances to deductions, you repay the *tax* on the amount of the disallowances, not the amount disallowed.

Rewrites

Sometimes a determination is not possible at the initial interview. If the examiner wants additional information, he may write up a "Request for Additional Information." This letter gives you fifteen days to submit further substantiation or clarification. This letter isn't used a whole lot. They feel taxpayers will get the information in faster, or not bother at all, if they're faced with a report asking for additional tax. The report lists the items audited, the adjustments made, if any, then all the figuring by which they arrive at additional tax, as well as penalty and interest if applicable. The report has a cover letter with it, which tells you that you have thirty days to agree or disagree with the audit findings. If you agree, simply sign one copy of the report and return it with a check for the additional tax.

    But there may be several changes in determination due to new information you supply, and before the case is closed, there may be several subsequent versions of the report: "revised," "supplemental," "revised-supplemental," "pastoral-tragical," "historical-comical," and so forth. The IRS is usually very understanding and will allow you reasonable time to get more information to them. If, however, they think you're jerking them around, they can get testy.

Paying the Piper

Once a case finding additional tax due has gone to "Collection," you're in a whole new ball game. *These* folks can be quite nasty. The Collection department can be a juggernaut whose left hand knoweth not what the right hand doeth. I've seen instances when a tax has been paid to an IRS Service Center and the local district Collection office is busy selling off the TV and the live stock. If you get involved with the Collection office, *always* write down the names of the people you talk to, either in person or on the phone, when you talked to them, and what they say. Keep a record of when you

make an installment payment and how much. There is as much as a six-week
lag between what the computer in the Service Center knows and what the
Collection department in your district knows. Most of the time, the best way
to deal with "Collection" is to present yourself live, in person, and bring canceled checks for them to photocopy if you need to prove that you have made
payment. NEVER let anyone keep original documents. They have photo-
copiers. After a tax is assessed, comes a series of ever-more-menacing letters
the last of which is the dread "Final Notice Before Seizure." If you get one
of these, cancel all other recreation for the day and get down there and find
out what went wrong, or make a payment, whichever is appropriate.

A New Production

Let's assume now that you don't like what an examiner has done to you in
an audit—don't like what he has disallowed or the reason something was
disallowed. Don't sign the report! Don't sign anything! You don't have to.
If you are told that you must sign the report, you are being lied to. If you
are told, "If you don't sign the report and I have to redo it, I'm afraid I won't
be able to be so generous; it will be harder on you." That's extortion.

You have a right to be told why something has been disallowed. If it
was because of inadequate substantiation, see if you can obtain better
proof. If it is because you have no basis for the deduction, there is nothing
you can do. If it is because of a difference in interpretation of something
and the examiner is adamant and immune to your brilliant rebuttal, you
must now resort to appeal procedures.

You can ask to see the examiner's group supervisor, in order to settle
the issues informally on that level. Group supervisors are more experienced
and sometimes less picky. They've seen more returns like yours and may
not think your return is so outrageous. On the other hand, they may be the
source of the examiner's attitude. A lot of "policy" is made on the group
level by supervisors.

If you don't get anywhere with the supervisor, tell him or her that you
want to have an Appellate Division conference. But, don't bother to appeal unless you have a case based on an *issue* and feel that you have a good
basis for the deduction. Otherwise, pay.

After an Appellate Division conference, there are various levels of
court actions you may take including: Small Claims Version (Small Tax
Case), Tax Court, District Court, Circuit Court. When you reach these
heights, you should have counsel, although you can represent yourself. If
you cannot afford legal counsel, contact Volunteer Lawyers for the Arts.
If the issue is one of a professional nature, as opposed to nonbusiness deductions such as "medical," and if you are destitute, they'll help you pre-

pare your appeal. However, the overwhelming majority of artists' returns can be examined and settled in the lower echelons.

A great many taxpayers get screwed because they don't know what they are doing and they are told less than the truth by IRS examiners. Yes, Virginia, there are some less-than-scrupulous examiners as well as some incompetent examiners at IRS. If you are ever in doubt about whether you've gotten a fair deal, just *don't sign* anything until you've had a chance to check things out. If you end up paying a tax you believe is excessive or erroneous, you can file a "Claim for Refund." If the claim is denied, you can file a refund suit in the U.S. District Court of Claims.

The Run of the Show

The limitation on time to assess additional tax is three years.* There are exceptions to that, but they probably don't apply to you or most freelance professionals. *Just keep your receipts for three years.* You can usually expect you won't be audited on a given year if you are not called in within twenty-one or twenty-two months after the due date of the return or the date it was filed, whichever is later. This period of time is called the audit cycle, and its length varies according to the workload in a given district. At any rate, they can get you for three years.

Keeping Your Scrapbook

Because they can get you for three years, keep your stuff for three years from the due date of the return or the date filed, whichever is later. But I suggest you review the Hobby Loss matter on page 14.

Nota bene! Items of equipment that are depreciating over a period of time appear on more than one return. The receipt for such an item must be kept for three years from the due date or the date filed of the last return on which the item appears as a deduction.

There are other limitation periods for entities other than individuals, such as corporations, but if you are a corporation, why are you reading this book?

Extending the Run

The IRS cannot extend the period of limitations on assessments without cause. In other words, if they think you've been up to no good, the law allows them to extend the period. Sometimes they will ask a taxpayer to sign a waiver extending the period for two years. Unless you've got a consid-

---

*The statute of limitations in your *state* may be longer; check it out.

ered reason for not signing—and I suggest that you get your considered reason from a tax attorney—sign the waiver. You haven't anything to hide, have you?

You should save audit reports and "no-change" letters because:

1. You have to report Federal audit changes to your state if you have a state income tax.
2. No-change letters can help expedite the repetitive audit program in your behalf.

CAUTION!

Never, never ignore correspondence from the IRS or any other taxing jurisdiction! If you're on the road and someone is picking up your mail, make sure they send any tax correspondence to you as soon as possible. If you don't understand what the letter means, CWYTP. If you don't have a tax preparer, call Taxpayer's Assistance at the nearest local IRS office. Check the white pages under "U.S. Government."

IRS Inspection Service

The following notice is reprinted from the *Boston District Tax Practitioner Newsletter:*

The integrity of the Federal income tax system depends on the integrity of Internal Revenue Service employees, tax professionals and taxpayers. Practitioners should be aware that the IRS Inspection Service is the place to report incidents of fraud, *abuse of power* [emphasis added], waste of government resources, bribery or any other suspicions of integrity lapses.

Inspection employees can be reached by telephone or by writing to the Service. A toll-free hotline, 1-800-366-4484, is located in Washington and connects directly to the IRS Inspection Service. Inspectors receive calls weekdays between the hours of 8:00 A.M. and 4:30 P.M. EST. Calls placed after business hours are recorded and returned by inspectors on the next working day.

Calls can also go to local IRS inspection Offices:

Washington,DC	(202) 566-4800
Cincinnati,OH	(513) 684-3562
Philadelphia, PA	(215) 597-0928

Lisle,IL	(708) 719-7930
N.Y., N.Y.	(212) 264-9130
Atlanta, GA	(404) 986-6900
Dallas, TX	(214) 308-1371
San Francisco, CA	(415) 744-9131

Although callers are encouraged to give their names, calls can *(sic)* be made anonymously.

If preferred, write directly to:
IRS Chief Inspector
P.O. Box 589
Washington, DC 20044-0589

7

Tax Preparers

Because I am a tax practitioner, I naturally feel that we are, by and large, a marvelous breed. At least those of us who are associated with artists are. Well, at least those of us associated with artists and writing this book are.

Should *you* go to a tax preparer? Unless you are willing to wade through a lot of government publications, and the one or two good self-help manuals on the market for preparing your own return, I would say you should go to a tax preparer. Of course, if you make a really small income in any particular year, you should try doing one of the two so-called "short forms," if you qualify, and try to get the money back yourself. You might use one of the tax equivalents of the fast-food restaurant. And by all means, you should try the A.E.A.–S.A.G. VITA* program, if you belong to either of those unions.

If you choose to use a tax preparer, be it a CPA or an experienced practitioner without a license, try to find a good one. So, define "good"! You cannot tell if a preparer is any good by the size of your refund. Size isn't everything. Big refunds and never getting audited are not the best criteria for determining a preparer's talent or knowledge.

A preparer should be willing to spend time with you. These characters who chat with you for ten minutes when you drop your stuff off had better ask a great many important questions during that ten-minute interview. If not, the job may be less than thorough. A good preparer should be available during the year to answer all your questions on the phone. Never hesitate to ask questions; the only stupid question is the one that doesn't get asked. After all, you're not supposed to be the sophisticate about taxes. You're not the one who is supposed to be reading and keeping current on taxes. A good tax person should be willing to help you prepare for an audit or actually represent you. I coach all my clients if they get audited, and they do very well, by and large.

Even considering the time pressures on preparers (we have to do the overwhelming majority of our work in the five or six weeks preceding April 15) you have a right to expect your return to be finished in a reasonable time after your initial interview. You can aid that cause by having all the necessary information on hand at the time of your appointment, so you don't have to have a second or third appointment, or be sending or calling in in-

*Volunteer Income Tax Assistance

formation at the last moment. Think about it: As April 15 draws nigh, suddenly everyone who was missing information in February or March sends or phones it in. During the last days of tax season, I practice triage: Those who will owe money get finished first. Their returns have to be filed by the fifteenth.

So, does your tax person take the time for you? I schedule an hour and a half for each appointment. Most returns can be done in this amount of time if the homework has been done and everything is in order. Has your preparer taken the time to explain record keeping, withholding exemptions, audit procedures, estimated tax, babies?

Tax preparers should treat the customers right, the same as anyone else in business. If you get short shrift, get another preparer. There are plenty of us around who like the Biz and understand being freelance and are eager to make a good living working for you all.

Make your preparer explain anything you don't understand on your return. Of course, this means you have to look the return over. If your preparer won't explain something or doesn't return your calls *ever,* spend your money elsewhere.

Beware of inventors! There is a queer breed in the land that feels its duty is get *your* taxable income to zero, even if that means inventing deductions. If you find a preparer has exaggerated your estimates or invented deductions, make the crook re-do the return at no extra cost. If you meet resistance, threaten to take the matter up with the IRS. After all it's you, the taxpayer, who is responsible for the information contained in your return. There is a statement printed over the place where you sign your return that reads: "Under penalties of perjury, I declare that I have examined this return, including accompanying schedules and statements, and to the best of my knowledge and belief it is *true, correct, and complete."* (Emphasis added.)

You are responsible—no one else.

Although it is true that you get what you pay for, high prices in and for themselves are no guarantee of good work. Most accountants charge by the hour. Some of us in the trade charge according to how much you make. I do. If you have a good year, I do, too. If you have a bad year, I charge you less. Satisfaction guaranteed. Any good tax person will give you your money's worth. I am available to my clients eleven months out of the year. Anyone who has a bad year financially gets the same TLC as when they've had a good year. There are preparers who try to confine their business to only "high rollers." They have an attitude problem.

Ethically, a preparer who makes a mistake on your return should reimburse any penalty or interest the mistake causes. Anyone can make a mistake, a math error, hit a wrong button on the adding machine. Because someone calls himself a tax preparer or an accountant doesn't mean he never makes mistakes. It does mean he should be willing to clean up the mess. To err is human; to forgive, divine; to pay penalty and interest goes with the territory.

If your preparer is expensive, make him earn his money. I tell my clients, "You've bought me for a year. Make me earn my fee." If you don't use your preparer to full advantage, you've no one to blame but yourself.

If you call me at home, I'll kill you. Twice. And get someone to hurt you. I once got a call from a client. It was 10:30 on a Friday night. I had guests lingering over coffee. She "just had one quick question." Did I think she should invest her money in numismatics? . . . So, take two aspirin, get plenty of rest and fluids, and call me at my *office* a year from October.

I adore all my clients except one, and I know that someday, one of my clients will step up to accept a Tony, or an Oscar, or a Nobel, and announce, "I owe it all to my parents, my coach, and my tax preparer!"

8

Plot Synopsis

1. You keep and/or are supplied with records of earned and non-earned income. You make estimates during the year and determine exactly, at year's end, your "gross income" for the year.

2. You keep good substantiation for various business and nonbusiness deductions.

Using the information acquired in steps no. 1 and no. 2, you determine whether you have to file quarterly Estimated Tax returns by April 15.

3. By April 15 each year (you can file later without penalty or interest if you owe no money), file Federal, State and City Individual Income Tax returns, which you have prepared by setting down your

- GROSS INCOME, from which you subtract "Adjustments," which gives you your
- ADJUSTED GROSS INCOME, from which you subtract the standard or itemized deductions and exemptions, and now you have your
- NET TAXABLE INCOME, on which you calculate your
- TAX LIABILITY, which may consist of more than one tax. Then you subtract credits and you have what is called your
- TOTAL TAX, which will be higher or lower than your
- PREPAYMENTS AND REFUNDABLECREDITS, which means there is either a
- TAX DUE, which means you have to file and pay by April 15 to avoid penalty and interest; or there will be an
- OVERPAYMENT, in which case you elect a
- REFUND, or you may have the overpayment
- CREDITED TO ESTIMATED TAX, for the following year.

4. You will then maintain your records of income and expenses for *at least three years* from the due date of the return or the date you file, whichever is later, against the possibility of an audit examination. *But* if you follow my advice, you will keep copies of returns and your diaries indefinitely. You may find yourself in a "hobby loss" fight with the IRS and need to prove "profit motive." Without a record of your career to date that might be impossible to do.*

*See page 14, 2nd paragraph.

Glossary

Adjustments to Income Certain expenses that you can subtract from gross income before you decide whether to itemize or take the standard deduction.

Adjusted Gross Income Gross income minus adjustments. Sometimes called AGI.

Assessment A bill for taxes.

Audit An examination of your return to verify income and deductions.

CWYTP An acronym of my own invention; it stands for Check With Your Tax Preparer.

Deductions Various business and nonbusiness expenses that can be subtracted from AGI, *q.v.,* in the process of arriving at net taxable income.

Dependents People who qualify as your dependent get you one "exemption" each. To qualify as your dependent, a person must meet the following five tests:

(1) *Support test.* You must furnish more than half the person's support for the year. *Note:* Divorced or separated parents or persons who participate in a joint support system for someone (for example, an aged parent), CWYTP!

(2) *Gross income test.* Normally, you cannot claim as a dependent any person who has gross taxable income of $2,450 during the year. There are two exceptions: (a) your child under 19 years of age, provided all the other tests are met; (b) your child of any age if a fulltime student (five or more months per year in a school).

(3) *Member of household or relationship test.* A member of your household need not be related to you, but must

81

live with you for the entire year. Temporary absences for vacation, school, sickness, etc., will not preclude the person from meeting this test. The test will not be met if you and the person in question are living together in violation of any state or local statutes forbidding cohabitation. A relative, on the other hand, need not live with you, but must be related in one of the following degrees: child, grandchild, great-grandchild (adopted or other), stepchild, brother, sister, half-brother, half-sister, step-brother, step-sister, [half-fish, half-human] parent, grand-parent, or any other direct ancestor, step-parent (but not foster parent), niece or nephew, father-in-law, mother-in-law, son-in-law, daughter-in-law, brother-in-law, or sister-in-law. (Whew!) If these relationships have once been established by marriage, they will not, for tax purposes, be abolished by divorce or death.

(4) *Citizenship test.*   The person must be a citizen or a resident of the United States, a resident of Canada, Mexico, the Republic of Panama, or the Canal Zone.

(5) *Joint-return test.*   The person cannot be one of the parties filing a joint return.

Estimated Tax   This is do-it-yourself withholding and prepayment of income and/or self-employment tax for the self-employed and certain other taxpayers with an expected tax liability of $500 or more, due to receipt of nontaxable income (investment income or alimony, for example). Estimated taxes must be paid quarterly. (See page 12)

Examination   1. Take a plain piece of lined paper and number 1 to 20 down the left side. Put your name, home room, and date in the upper-left corner.
2. See **Audit.**

Exclusion   An amount of money excluded from computation of taxable income.

Exemption   An amount of money exempted from taxation. You get one exemption for yourself and one for each dependent when you compute your next taxable income.

Fees   1. Payments to independent contractors. No taxes are withheld from fees, and estimated taxes may have to be paid quarterly. Fees are reported on 1099-MISC forms. 2. See *f* spelled backward.

FICA *"Federal Insurance Contributions Act."* This regards Social Security and Medicare.

Filing If your marital status at the end of the year is "single," your
Status income tax filing status is "single" and you pay tax at a different rate on the same income as a married couple filing jointly, filing separately, or a head-of-a-household, or a qualified widow or widower with a dependent child, etc.

Forms and NOTE: You can get any tax form you want by dialing 1-
Schedules 800-TAX-FORM. Just tell the nice machine what form you want and if you don't know the form number, say what you want it to do. But keep in mind it will take 30 days. Maybe you should just go to the IRS office.

(1) *W-2* The form your employer must send you at year's end to report earnings and withholding from wages, salaries, tips, and "other compensation."

(2) *W-4* When you start a job, you fill out a W-4 so the payroll department will withhold the correct amount for your filing status and exemptions.

(3) *1099-Misc* Used to report fees, commissions, rents, royalties, etc.; nonemployee compensation.

(4) *1099-Int* Reports interest earned.
1099-Div Reports dividends earned.
1099-B Reports proceeds from real estate, broker, and barter-exchange transactions.
1099-G Reports government payments: refunds, unemployment, etc.

(5) *K-1* reports income or (loss) from partnerships, estates, trusts, and small business corporations to you and the IRS.

(6) *1040A* The "short form." It is used to file individual tax returns when the only income is from wages, salaries, tips, unemployment, interest and dividends. You can take no adjustments or deductions except IRAs and your total income must be less than $50,000.

(7) *1040EZ* The *other* short form! It is used to file individual returns if you are single, under 65, with total taxable income under $50,000 consisting of only wages, salaries, tips, and not more than $400 in taxable interest. You cannot be blind or take any adjustments or deductions.

(8) *1040*   The "long form." It is used to file all individual tax returns disqualified from using 1040A or 1040EZ.

(9) *Schedule A*   Used to claim itemized deductions and is attached to 1040.

(10) *Schedule B*   Used to report dividend and/or interest income of more than $400 each. Attached to Form 1040.

(11) *Schedule C*   For reporting income and expenses of a self-employed person (sole proprietor). Attached to Form 1040.

(12) *Schedule D*   For reporting sale or exchange of capital assets and property. Attached to Form 1040.

(13) *Schedule E*   Used to report income from partnerships, estates, trusts, and small business corporations. Attached to Form 1040.

(14) *Schedule ES*   Used to compute and file quarterly estimated tax returns.

(15) *Schedule SE*   Used to compute self-employment tax. Attached to Form 1040.

(16) *Form 1116*   Used to compute the credit for tax paid to a foreign country. Attached to Form 1040.

(17) *Form 2106*   Used to claim employee business expenses. Attached to Form 1040.

(18) *Form 2441*   Used to calculate credit for child and dependent care. Attached to Form 1040.

(19) *Form 3903*   Used to claim employee moving expenses. Attached to Form 1040.

(20) *Form 4137*   Used to compute social security tax on unreported tip income. Attached to Form 1040.

(21) *Form 8829*   Used to claim deduction for business use of residence.

(22) *Document 5635*   Used to report tip income to your employer. It includes forms 4070 and 4070A to aid in record keeping and reporting said income.

(23) *Form 8283*   Used to claim any non-cash charitable contribution of more than $500.

(24) Form 9465   Used to request an installment payment arrangement when you cannot pay your final tax tab on the dread day in April.

This is, of course, a partial list only but consists of the most commonly used forms and schedules. (At least as far as you are concerned, Dear Reader.)

Other Compensation In the Biz, this is most often transportation money, wardrobe allowance, or some other payment not subject to Social Security tax.

Overpayment The excess of prepayments and refundable credits over tax liability. (See also **Refund**, below.) You can either take the refund or have the overpayment credited to your payments for the following year, if you will be liable for estimated taxes.

Rebop Not dealt with in this book.

Refund An overpayment of taxes returned to you. If you elect a refund and do not receive it within two months, write a follow-up letter, giving your social security number, the date you filed, and a request that a tracer be put on the check.

Return (1) The papers you file with taxing authorities to report your income, deductions, etc
(2) A misnomer for "refund."

Salary A form of financial remuneration regularly received and having taxes withheld. Salary is the weekly or annual version of wages.

Tax Home Your principal place of business, where you reside, vote, worship, pay taxes, etc. Tax Court has said that substantial living expenses must be incurred at a permanent place of abode in order to claim that place as a tax home (Christy, Richard, TC Memo 1993–156).

Tips Oh, come on! You know what tips are. We're not concerned here with ones like: "Pensioner in the fifth at Belmont!" Get serious, Lype. But you should see Item #22 under "Forms and Schedules."

Untaxed This frequently used vernacular term has no real meaning, but is commonly used to mean "unwithheld." It should not be confused with "nontaxable," which means completely exempted from taxation.

Wages Hourly remuneration from which taxes are withheld. (See **Salary.**)

Withholding The method by which your employer prepays your income tax and social security tax. By submitting a W-4 form you dictate how much tax the employer should take out. You should keep a weather eye on your paycheck stubs to see that the correct taxes are being taken out. I mean correct both as to amount and jurisdiction. If you go on a tour, your home state and city taxes should still be taken out. Sometimes a second state will be dipping into the pay envelope. That's legal! If you see little or no tax being taken out, better find out why and do something about it. If you have to, protest!

A Short List of Some Helpful IRS Publications

Publication Name	Number
Business Expenses	535
Business Use of a Car	917
Business Use of Your Home	587
Charitable Contributions	526
Child and Dependent Care Credit, and Employment Taxes for Household Employers	503
Credit for the Elderly or for the Totally and Permanently Disabled	524
Depreciation	534
Determining the Value of Donated Property	561
Earned Income Credit	596
Educational Expenses	508
Employee's Daily Record of Tips (Form 4070-A) and Employee's Report of Tips to Employer (Form 4070)	1244
Examination of Returns, Appeal Rights, and Claims for Refund	556
Exemptions and Standard Deduction	501
Foreign Tax Credit for U.S. Citizens and Resident Aliens	514
Guide to Free Tax Services	910
Individual Retirement Arrangements (IRSs)	590
Is My Withholding Correct for (tax year)	919
Medical and Dental Expenses	502
Miscellaneous Deductions	529
Moving Expenses	521
New Rules for Home Mortgage Interest Deduction	932
Reporting Income from Tips	531
Scholarships and Fellowships	520
Self-Employed Retirement Plans	560
Self-Employment Tax	533

Publication Name	Number
Tax Guide for Small Business	334
Tax Guide for U.S. Citizens and Resident Aliens Abroad	54
Tax Information for Divorced or Separated Individuals	504
Tax Information on Selling Your Home	523
Tax Rules for Children and Dependents	929
Tax Withholding and Estimated Tax	505
Taxable and Nontaxable Income	525
Travel, Entertainment, and Gift Expenses	463
Your Federal Income Tax	17

Form W-4

In what film does Alan Ladd say (without any apparent movement of an articulator, by the way), "A gun is only a tool, Marian. 'sno better or worse than the man using it."?

As soon as I get through writing this book, I'm resuming work on the screenplay for the first Kasha Western, *Schoen!*

The scene is Graftman's Dairy Restaurant in the Negev. In the corner, sipping ein gless seltzer, is a wicked awesome dude in a burnoose and mirror sunglasses: Jake Willsohn. Leaning against the pastry case is our hero, Schoen. Schoen breaks the silence . . .

SCHOEN: So, you're Jake Willsohn? (He pronounces it: Villson.)

WILLSOHN: Det's right, Schoen!

SCHOEN: I hoid o' you.

WILLSOHN: So, vot did you hear, Schoen?

SCHOEN: I hoid you vas a terrorist!

WILLSOHN: So, sue me!

A W-4 is only a tool, Marian; no better and no worse than the actor filling it out. Filling one out is not all that difficult as far as the mechanics are concerned, if you are a normal person. But no one here is normal, as far as I can tell. So, you need some help. So, here comes some! You can't be too careful where you get your help. Would you let a stage manager or your agent remove your appendix? If you would, let them fill in your W-4 for you. You really have to do it yourself. Of course, you can CWYTP.

The IRS frequently revises Form W-4, but the basic idea remains the same. Call the IRS and ask them to send you a half a dozen or so copies and practice on one till you get the idea. Save the rest and photocopy them as needed when you want to amend your withholding by increasing or decreasing exemptions. If you get a high-paying role and you have a small income from a commercial—say, holding fees—and they're not taking anything out, you can just go ahead and submit an amended W-4 to T&R, or whomever, as the year goes on and not find out the following April that you're under-withheld.

The general idea of the form is to allow you to adjust the amount of withholding from your salary so that at year's end *you don't owe them and they don't owe you.* Correct use of a W-4 allows you to get your "refund" every week in your take-home pay. Some people like to be over-withheld so that they get a big refund, so they put zero exemptions. Others like to bank the money as the year goes on, collect some interest, and then file their return with a balance due. Of course, if you do this, you have to be sure to get your return in by April 15 to avoid penalty and interest to the Fed and state. This is okay to a point, but if you owe enough, there'll still be penalty and interest even if you file on time.

Under the law, taxpayers are not allowed to claim an excessive number of withholding exemptions simply because they need the money. Employers are required to forward to the IRS any W-4s claiming more than ten exemptions (as of 1988).

I encourage my clients to call me and ask for help when confronted with the formidable W-4. "How many exemptions can I put down?" There's a different answer for each person and for each time of the year. If I have certain information, I can help. I need to know:

1. How much money have you *grossed* and do you reasonably expect to gross this year? Earned and nonearned income.
2. How many exemptions have you been putting down? It's a good idea to keep track of that on that same list discussed in Appendix III.
3. How much have you had withheld so far for Fed, state, and local tax.
4. What are your deductions looking like this year? Have a look at last year's return as an aid to estimating that.

Let me try a couple of scenarios on you. Say you got a job on a TV movie. Your gross is $3,000 per week for two weeks. The withholding on $3,000 is going to be high, as if you're making $152,000 per year. If the only other income you have that year is unemployment, you're going to be way over-withheld. This extreme case calls for the maximum exemptions and part-year withholding method discussed a little farther down the line.

Another example, a state of affairs that can be insulting as well as expensive: You're getting lots of small checks from many sources. You've got several holding fees, many small residual checks, Off-Broadway salary, a modest bread-and-butter job. You are grossing $600 a week, average, but the average of the several checks in a week is $310. On top of it, you've got seven exemptions down on all the jobs. Maybe if any one of the jobs was your only job you wouldn't owe any money, BUT the sum of the taxes on the parts is not equal to and falls short of the tax on the total. Did you follow that? If you experience this, as the year wears on you'd better submit an amended W-4 directing them to take out extra money. That's kosher.

Try to keep a running tab on your weekly gross, know what it is, know what you are averaging, and if someone pays you a weekly wage that is less than that, claim FEWER exemptions; if more than you have been averaging, claim MORE exemptions up to the maximum of *ten.* Get it? Do not do the opposite without being prepared to take the consequences. *The more you make, the more you can claim; the less you make, the fewer you should claim.*

So what about those dream jobs that pay thousands per week? Well, if you're going to get several thousand dollars a week for many weeks, you are going to have to pay a lot of tax, so put one for yourself, your agent, the job, your expenses, and the bairns, etc. If you claim all your exemptions on one job, you cannot legally claim them on every job. So claim them on the high-paying jobs.

Let's say your dream job is lasting two weeks. In the middle of September you get cast as the shicksa in *Schoen* for $5,000 for two weeks. (That's ten grand!) Even ten exemptions ain't gonna help. They're gonna murder those checks. And after your agent deducts his pound, and your manager, God forbid, a pound and a half, you're left with zip. Ah, musha-mush! Ochone! (That's Irish for "God Almighty, Scarlett!")

Never fear. Help is on the way. Publication 539 *(Employment Taxes)* tells us that if along with your W-4 you submit a *written* request for the part-year withholding method, your employer may comply. The written request must state therein:

1. The number of weeks you have worked for any other employer during the year including the one(s) in question and the last date you worked for this employer or any other employer last in the current year.
2. That you use the calendar-year accounting period. (Just shut up and do it!)
3. That you will not work more than 245 days during the current calendar year.

It works like this: Let's say you've been out of work for thirteen weeks. Add that to the two weeks you worked on *Schoen* and you get FIFTEEN WEEKS. If the payroll department is asked to do so, they may divide the $10,000 received (2 [weeks] x $5,000) by 15, and come up with $666.67 per week. Then they determine the withholding on that amount, and multiply it by 15 weeks. Let's say a person has four exemptions—a personal exemption and three well-considered additional withholding allowances. This means a weekly deduction of $94 and a total Federal Withholding Tax of $1,410 (15 x $94) for the fifteen-week period. The withholding on $5,000 a week for the same person on a two-week basis would be $1,404.71 per week, or $2,809.42 for two weeks. So, you see, it can really save your hide if the employer will do part-year withholding. Otherwise you just get this humungous refund, which might arrive after you've starved to death. Part-year withholding is also good on state and city income taxes but not state or local "gross" or "wage" taxes, where they just take out a flat percentage anyway, so it makes no difference to your take-home.

It's not easy, this W-4 business, but remember, if you estimate as the year goes along that you may be over- or under-withheld, you are allowed by law to amend your withholding allowances by submitting a new Form W-4. Of course, your employer may find you a pain in the tush. Como se dice "tush" in Inglese?

Read the fine print just above the space provided for your signature on Form W-4. They mean it!

The Parting Glass

Everything preceding this is arguable and subject to interpretation, not to mention congressional whimsy.

If you take issue or are disappointed with anything herein, the author is sorry. If you find any errors or believe there are serious omissions, he welcomes hearing of them, as well as receiving any suggestions as to how to keep this the best book of its kind on the market, which it has been and always will continue to be. Beware of cheap imitations and knock-offs!

Brendan says, *"Go raibh mile maith agat."*

Appendix I
Typical Price List from a Thrift Store
of a Group Featured in a Shaw Play

The following is a list of the average prices charged for items in *good* condition. New or expensive items would be higher and damaged items less. This list is for your guidance only. There are, of course, variables such as condition, age, antique value, cleanliness, and value when new. An appraisal is recommended for items in excess of $200.00. The following paragraph is a paraphrase from IRS Pub. 526 which explains the requirement that a contributor attach to his or her income tax return the following information* if a donation of goods exceeds $500.00:

1) Name and address of the organization to which the donation was made.
2) Date of contribution.
3) Description of property including condition.
4) Cost of property.
5) Fair market value and method used to determine same.
6) Amount claimed as a deduction.

Additional information is required for *any single item* deducted with a value in excess of $100.00

*By using form 8283.

LADIES' CLOTHING	LOW	HIGH	MEN'S CLOTHING	LOW	HIGH
Bathing suits	4.00	20.00	Jackets	15.00	50.00
Bathrobes	5.00	30.00	Overcoats	25.00	150.00
Blouses	5.00	25.00	Raincoats	25.00	75.00
Boots	5.00	50.00	Shirts	5.00	15.00
Coats	15.00	150.00	Shoes	5.00	50.00
Dresses	10.00	100.00	Shorts	2.00	10.00
Evening dresses	50.00	400.00	Slacks	5.00	20.00
Hand bags	5.00	50.00	Suits	30.00	100.00
Hats and Gloves	1.00	10.00	Sweaters	5.00	35.00
Lingerie	1.00	20.00	Swim trunks	2.50	5.50
Pants suits	10.00	60.00	Tuxedos	40.00	100.00
Shoes	5.00	50.00	Underwear	1.00	5.00
Skirts	5.00	35.00			
Slacks	5.00	35.00			
Socks and Belts	1.00	5.00			
Suits	15.00	100.00			
Sweaters	5.00	25.00			

FURS AND ANTIQUES PER APPRAISAL

CHILDREN'S CLOTHING	LOW	HIGH
Blouses	1.00	15.00
Dresses	5.00	30.00
Jackets	3.00	20.00
Jeans	3.50	8.50
Shirts	1.00	15.00
Skirts	1.00	15.00
Slacks	1.00	15.00
Snow suits and Coats	5.00	25.00
Suits, boys	5.00	30.00

FURNITURE	LOW	HIGH
Air conditioners	25.00	125.00
Bed and accessories	50.00	275.00
Bicycles	15.00	45.00
Carriages	5.00	100.00
Chests	25.00	45.00
Convertible sofas	75.00	600.00
Desk	25.00	175.00
Dresser Armoire	50.00	350.00
Dryer (working)	50.00	150.00
Floor lamps	5.00	150.00
Gas stoves	50.00	225.00
High chairs	10.00	35.00
Kitchen cabinets	25.00	75.00
Kitchen chairs	5.00	50.00
Play pens	7.50	20.00
Refrigerators	75.00	600.00
Rug, area	40.00	300.00
Sewing machines	40.00	100.00
Sofas	50.00	600.00
Tables	5.00	300.00
Televisions	35.00	300.00
Typewriters	20.00	150.00
Upholstered chairs	10.00	300.00
Vacuum cleaners	25.00	100.00
Washing machines	50.00	200.00

COMPLETE SETS	LOW	HIGH
Bedroom set	250.00	800.00
Dining room set	150.00	650.00
Kitchen set	35.00	325.00

DRY GOODS	LOW	HIGH
Bed spread	10.00	50.00
Blanket	5.00	10.00
Curtain	2.00	10.00
Drapes	20.00	100.00
Pillow	1.00	5.00
Sheet	2.00	5.50
Throw rug	1.50	4.50
Towel	1.00	3.00

Appendix II
Record of Earned Income
"List, list, O list"——Hamlet, I, iv

Always inform payers when you move. Although residual checks are sent to SAG, do not assume that SAG informs producers and paymaster companies that you have a new address. W-2 forms are not sent to SAG. If you haven't kept tally of your various employers and residual payments as the year wears on, you won't be able to tell if you have all your W-2's by mid-February (which is when you should be filing). It can be very difficult to know who owes you a W-2 because properties are sold, payroll companies merge, etc. List, list, O list and you may save yourself a lot of aggravation later. Getting a CP 2000 letter from IRS demanding more tax and interest because you forgot an employer or two is no fun.

Date on Check	Date Rec'd.	Product or Production Name	Producer or Theatre

Payroll Company if Applicable	Gross	Net Amount	Commission (Y or N)	Number of Exemptions

Date on Check	Date Rec'd.	Product or Production Name	Producer or Theatre

Appendix III
Automobile Mileage Between Cities

"Wherever the four winds blow . . . "
Johnny Mercer (with Harold Arlen)

TO \ FROM	Albany, N. Y.	Atlanta—Ga.	Baltimore, Md.	Boston, Mass.	Buffalo, N. Y.	Chicago, Ill.	Cincinnati, Ohio	Cleveland, Ohio	Columbus, Ohio	Dallas, Tex.	Denver, Colo.	Detroit, Mich.	Houston, Tex.	Indianapolis, Ind.	Kansas City, Mo.
Albany, N. Y.	.....	1068	*331*	*171*	*278*	803	701	462	603	1717	1835	*530*	1829	*757*	1278
Amarillo, Tex.	1817	1150	1669	1983	1501	1098	1136	1333	1207	362	438	1305	605	1033	583
Asheville, N. C.	890	230	504	*900*	755	647	359	585	437	999	1539	608	1061	464	902
Atlanta, Ga.	1068	.....	687	1083	914	707	472	726	580	814	1495	734	848	554	844
Baltimore, Md.	*331*	687	.....	*399*	353	685	502	*351*	395	1436	1617	*511*	1521	568	1062
Birmingham, Ala.	1223	155	842	1228	939	667	497	751	605	659	1376	759	713	507	738
Bismarck, N. D.	*1694*	1586	1563	1873	1403	866	1153	1215	1171	1196	793	1153	1470	1042	816
Boise, Idaho	2648	2288	2426	2807	2337	1820	1970	2449	2119	1684	884	1987	1877	1860	1444
Boston, Mass.	*171*	1083	399	.....	*447*	*972*	882	631	772	1837	2021	*699*	1928	*926*	1444
Buffalo, N. Y.	*278*	914	353	*447*	.....	527	425	186	327	1421	1551	252	1533	*481*	984
Calgary, Alta.	2555	2496	2404	2714	2280	1727	2008	2056	2026	1916	1116	1994	2159	1917	1645
Charleston, W. Va.	*683*	529	406	795	457	488	211	268	174	1111	1434	362	1238	321	790
Chattanooga, Tenn.	1052	120	660	1085	791	589	349	603	457	799	1368	611	861	434	731
Cheyenne, Wyo.	1817	1525	1663	1962	1492	975	1207	1318	1271	903	103	1242	1146	1097	694
Chicago, Ill.	*803*	707	*685*	*972*	*527*	.....	324	*341*	359	957	1034	*293*	1110	184	507
Cincinnati, Ohio	*701*	472	502	*882*	425	324	.....	239	106	960	1161	255	1102	109	*601*
Cleveland, Ohio	*462*	726	*351*	*631*	*186*	*341*	239	.....	141	1233	1363	*167*	1356	295	794
Colorado Spgs, Colo.	1875	1463	1672	2088	1583	1095	1213	1395	1282	731	69	1382	974	1106	612
Columbia, S. C.	854	218	512	903	852	811	565	664	538	1032	1695	781	1102	637	1058
Columbus, Ohio	*603*	580	*395*	772	*327*	359	106	141	.....	1068	1225	185	1210	173	670
Dallas, Tex.	1717	814	1436	1837	1421	957	960	1233	1068	.....	800	1200	243	933	521
Denver, Colo.	1835	1495	1617	2021	1551	1034	1161	1363	1225	800	.....	1321	1043	1051	644
Des Moines, Ia.	1152	945	1038	1331	881	344	578	673	664	736	691	611	973	468	209
Detroit, Mich.	*530*	734	*511*	*699*	252	*293*	255	*167*	185	1200	1321	.....	1307	277	766
Duluth, Minn.	1324	1203	1193	1503	974	496	797	847	815	1147	1072	756	1428	686	620
El Paso, Tex.	2237	1441	2063	2400	1941	1515	1556	1753	1627	627	721	1725	750	1453	1000
Evansville, Ind.	998	413	769	*1104*	678	297	236	490	344	764	1075	436	881	164	431
Fargo, N. D.	-1498	1390	1367	1677	1207	670	957	1019	975	1136	955	957	1379	846	669
Ft. Smith, Ark.	1422	696	1272	1602	1126	710	741	938	849	295	815	910	497	638	309
Ft. Wayne, Ind.	*674*	*667*	*556*	*843*	*398*	175	151	*212*	154	1046	1161	161	1148	116	607
Galveston, Tex.	1877	896	1550	1957	1592	1160	1150	1404	1258	293	1093	1355	50	1007	814
Great Falls, Mont.	2366	2174	2235	2525	1981	1538	1809	1867	1837	1556	756	1805	1799	1699	1323
Greensboro, N. C.	*675*	352	320	716	688	786	*479*	536	442	1166	1686	630	1254	*589*	1042
Harrisburg, Pa.	*338*	762	74	*398*	284	655	484	321	382	1469	1695	*481*	1582	*556*	1046
Hartford, Conn.	*109*	1011	*301*	*104*	*393*	*918*	784	577	682	1736	1974	*645*	1827	*863*	1357
Helena, Mont.	2379	2197	2246	2536	2066	1549	1832	1878	1846	1612	812	1826	1855	1722	1346
Houston, Tex.	1829	868	1521	1928	1533	1110	1102	1356	1210	243	1043	1307	.....	1035	764
Indianapolis, Ind.	*757*	554	568	*926*	*481*	184	109	295	173	933	1051	277	1035	.....	494
Jacksonville, Fla.	1165	324	799	1198	1187	1036	796	962	875	1024	1789	1063	958	881	1175
Kansas City, Mo.	1278	844	1062	1444	984	507	601	794	670	521	644	766	764	494	.....
Knoxville, Tenn.	911	192	548	944	722	568	280	534	388	890	1427	542	973	373	790
Las Vegas, Nev.	2756	2024	2519	2915	2424	1887	2010	2236	2225	1251	914	2174	1501	1951	1457
Lexington, Ky.	*875*	387	598	*987*	527	372	85	339	193	919	1242	347	1036	188	*598*
Lincoln, Neb.	1369	1076	1197	1535	1058	548	741	882	805	640	493	809	883	631	225
Little Rock, Ark.	1403	542	1101	1502	1081	661	665	893	756	335	967	865	452	593	408
Los Angeles, Cal.	2941	2257	2793	3107	2645	2175	2260	2457	2331	1443	1265	2429	1566	2157	1728
Louisville, Ky.	*870*	440	641	*976*	550	305	108	362	216	852	1168	370	994	114	524
Memphis, Tenn.	1273	403	962	1363	953	549	511	744	619	474	1103	716	591	444	466

Italics denote shortest routes using one or more turnpikes

FROM / TO	Los Angeles, Cal.	Louisville, Ky.	Memphis, Tenn.	Miami, Fla.	Minneapolis-St. Paul	New Orleans, La.	New York, N.Y.	Omaha, Neb.	Philadelphia, Pa.	Richmond, Va.	St. Louis, Mo.	Salt Lake City, Utah	San Francisco, Cal.	Seattle, Wash.	Washington, D.C.
Albany, N. Y.	2941	846	1273	1470	1242	1592	169	1310	236	507	1070	2276	3008	2979	369
Amarillo, Tex.	1124	1059	747	1736	1042	869	1789	678	1699	1616	792	899	1457	1789	1630
Asheville, N. C.	2396	371	525	773	1062	706	696	1054	604	383	638	2042	2729	2814	469
Atlanta, Ga.	2257	440	403	681	1122	524	875	1056	783	561	587	1991	2644	2773	648
Baltimore, Md.	2793	641	962	1159	1112	1211	187	1156	97	144	806	2122	2881	2849	38
Birmingham, Ala.	2102	394	244	796	1079	357	1030	950	938	719	548	1864	2440	2678	769
Bismarck, N. D.	1740	1156	1299	2267	437	1684	1720	604	1623	1654	999	1000	1759	1263	1559
Boise, Idaho	900	1968	1934	2993	1477	2141	2646	1270	2557	2492	1701	373	653	510	2506
Boston, Mass.	3107	976	1363	1550	1422	1609	216	1469	304	540	1239	2424	3187	3125	437
Buffalo, N. Y.	2645	550	953	1450	952	1296	445	999	366	512	797	1954	2717	2687	361
Calgary, Alta.	1624	2195	2135	3157	1329	2375	2553	1493	2464	2638	1889	889	1479	760	2400
Charleston, W. Va.	2449	266	647	1046	903	936	587	911	497	311	533	1877	2636	2656	367
Chattanooga, Tenn.	2196	320	325	801	1019	505	848	936	756	545	467	1871	2529	2653	621
Cheyenne, Wyo.	1194	1205	1231	2213	840	1400	1844	507	1750	1729	938	461	1218	1300	1740
Chicago, Ill.	2175	305	549	1388	415	941	841	482	760	788	294	1437	2200	2172	685
Cincinnati, Ohio	2260	108	511	1132	716	854	653	700	572	622	340	1666	2425	2435	492
Cleveland, Ohio	2457	362	744	1314	764	1108	507	811	426	479	611	1766	2529	2501	351
Colorado Spgs., Colo.	1172	1136	1018	2102	975	1238	1895	580	1768	1713	869	580	1339	1371	1671
Columbia, S. C.	2495	544	649	650	1227	724	700	1227	603	363	794	2198	2882	2980	468
Columbus, Ohio	2331	216	619	1210	734	962	551	764	470	485	411	1730	2492	2471	395
Dallas, Tex.	1443	852	474	1350	991	507	1629	679	1537	1341	641	1250	1800	2151	1402
Denver, Colo.	1265	1168	1103	2143	916	1297	1807	552	1712	1745	901	530	1270	1381	1614
Des Moines, Ia.	1840	625	620	1626	255	1023	1189	139	1086	1122	358	1105	1864	1844	1035
Detroit, Mich.	2429	370	716	1374	702	1116	667	750	586	650	560	1704	2467	2439	511
Duluth, Minn.	2174	800	977	1884	156	1377	1342	520	1253	1284	676	1439	2198	1713	1189
El Paso, Tex.	816	1476	1101	2001	1459	1135	2175	1095	2100	1968	1212	898	1241	1785	2029
Evansville, Ind.	2090	128	280	1085	712	683	918	643	828	705	174	1571	2330	2353	732
Fargo, N. D.	1925	960	1103	2058	241	1504	1516	457	1427	1458	803	1190	1949	1459	1363
Ft. Smith, Ark.	1581	664	290	1330	773	576	1394	521	1304	1159	397	1326	1914	2140	1233
Ft. Wayne, Ind.	2270	220	557	1340	576	960	712	646	631	639	354	1612	2371	2313	556
Galveston, Tex.	1616	1042	639	1316	1278	372	1749	972	1646	1435	861	1554	2041	2395	1468
Great Falls, Mont.	1323	1873	1811	2835	1007	2053	2384	1171	2275	2316	1567	588	1292	706	2231
Greensboro, N. C.	2584	618	713	837	1201	876	508	1179	416	230	785	2230	2947	2964	281
Harrisburg, Pa.	2740	598	995	1237	1072	1185	186	1143	105	219	794	2074	2833	2809	112
Hartford, Conn.	3020	897	1262	1490	1354	1472	118	1444	206	439	1185	2356	3119	3082	339
Helena, Mont.	1229	1894	1834	2871	1030	2007	2415	1192	2286	2317	1603	494	1128	617	2242
Houston, Tex.	1566	994	591	1300	1228	385	1675	922	1572	1406	813	1504	1991	2394	1482
Indianapolis, Ind.	2157	114	444	1235	605	847	724	590	643	632	238	1556	2315	2250	568
Jacksonville, Fla.	2467	764	671	356	1473	573	1031	1373	898	658	911	2287	2869	3101	763
Kansas City, Mo.	1728	524	466	1516	464	868	1220	212	1160	1101	257	1174	1899	1994	1059
Knoxville, Tenn.	2287	259	415	871	983	617	736	985	644	433	526	1930	2620	2712	509
Las Vegas, Nev.	289	1933	1621	2625	1729	1758	2707	1466	2617	2490	1666	446	596	1195	2504
Lexington, Ky.	2257	74	445	1068	787	769	779	810	681	503	341	1738	2497	2520	559
Lincoln, Neb.	1663	749	715	1757	423	1093	1369	59	1265	1263	482	928	1687	1697	1194
Little Rock, Ark.	1735	524	139	1176	836	460	1294	620	1198	1008	361	1478	2068	2294	1067
Los Angeles, Cal.	.....	2183	1871	2817	2018	1951	2913	1701	2823	2740	1916	735	408	1190	2754
Louisville, Ky.	2138	.....	385	1121	720	751	790	704	700	577	267	1664	2423	2446	604
Memphis, Tenn.	1871	385	.....	1030	863	403	1155	680	1059	869	301	1616	2204	2430	928

TO \ FROM	Albany, N. Y.	Atlanta—Ga.	Baltimore, Md.	Boston, Mass.	Buffalo, N. Y.	Chicago, Ill.	Cincinnati, Ohio	Cleveland, Ohio	Columbus, Ohio	Dallas, Tex.	Denver, Colo.	Detroit, Mich.	Houston, Tex.	Indianapolis, Ind.	Kansas City, Mo.
Miami, Fla.	1470	681	1159	1550	1450	1388	1132	1314	1210	1350	2143	1374	1300	1235	1516
Milwaukee, Wis.	891	796	773	1060	615	91	429	429	447	1046	1050	381	1199	279	596
Minneapolis-St. Paul.	1242	1122	1112	1422	952	415	716	764	734	991	916	702	1228	605	464
Mobile, Ala.	1433	365	1052	1448	1218	870	742	1030	850	599	1389	1038	537	748	853
Montgomery, Ala.	1245	177	864	1260	1030	767	588	842	696	659	1459	850	725	605	835
Montreal, Que.	228	1267	580	327	409	886	851	597	743	1808	1914	593	1900	855	1359
Nashville, Tenn.	1104	257	742	1138	775	451	291	587	399	694	1231	553	811	297	587
New Orleans, La.	1592	524	1211	1609	1296	941	854	1108	962	507	1297	1116	385	847	868
New York, N. Y.	169	875	187	216	445	841	653	507	551	1629	1807	667	1675	724	1220
Oklahoma City, Okla.	1555	888	1407	1721	1239	826	876	1071	945	211	618	1043	454	771	358
Omaha, Neb.	1310	1056	1156	1469	999	482	700	811	764	679	552	750	922	590	212
Philadelphia, Pa.	236	783	97	304	366	760	572	426	470	1537	1712	586	1572	643	1160
Phoenix, Ariz.	2525	1839	2405	2717	2255	1793	1872	2067	1941	1040	827	2013	1163	1767	1276
Pittsburgh, Pa.	492	752	230	598	220	459	284	125	182	1247	1410	285	1389	356	853
Portland, Me.	238	1188	501	105	530	1053	972	722	900	1942	2073	782	2067	1022	1516
Portland, Ore.	3073	2803	2935	3252	2768	2265	2478	2594	2564	2137	1337	2532	2385	2368	1952
Providence, R. I.	166	1083	366	43	450	975	849	634	747	1808	2056	801	1899	921	1429
Quebec, Que.	401	1440	753	402	582	1053	1024	743	884	1981	2087	766	2073	1028	1532
Raleigh, N. C.	645	402	303	699	671	866	559	616	522	1216	1766	710	1304	669	1122
Rapid City, S. D.	1770	1592	1619	1929	1459	942	1252	1271	1241	1134	406	1209	1402	1137	761
Richmond, Va.	507	561	144	540	512	788	522	479	485	1341	1745	650	1406	632	1101
Sacramento, Cal.	2919	2614	2792	3096	2626	2109	2336	2438	2403	1815	1181	2376	1961	2226	1810
St. Joseph, Mo.	1274	905	1056	1440	978	500	600	790	664	581	561	767	818	490	54
St. Louis, Mo.	1070	587	806	1239	797	294	340	611	411	641	901	560	813	238	257
Salt Lake City, Utah.	2276	1991	2122	2424	1954	1437	1666	1766	1730	1250	530	1704	1504	1556	1174
San Antonio, Tex.	2012	1098	1706	2104	1692	1251	1250	1504	1358	274	954	1474	196	1183	795
San Diego, Cal.	2912	2184	2768	3082	2620	2191	2235	2432	2306	1370	1192	2378	1493	2132	1682
San Francisco, Cal.	3008	2644	2881	3187	2717	2200	2425	2529	2492	1800	1270	2467	1991	2315	1899
Santa Fe, N. M.	2110	1430	1959	2276	1801	1378	1428	1613	1487	642	391	1585	885	1313	832
Sault Ste. Marie.	775	1074	899	940	553	491	604	513	530	1406	1453	352	1540	520	936
Scranton, Pa.	175	884	219	310	248	777	564	369	462	1570	1761	500	1712	635	1166
Seattle, Wash.	2979	2773	2849	3125	2687	2172	2435	2501	2471	2151	1381	2439	2394	2250	1994
Shreveport, La.	1623	627	1312	1713	1303	890	862	1115	969	187	977	1066	241	794	565
Sioux City, Ia.	1318	1149	1207	1497	1027	510	782	839	819	785	613	777	1028	672	318
Sioux Falls, S. D.	1396	1237	1265	1555	1085	568	870	897	867	873	695	835	1116	760	406
Spokane, Wash.	2684	2478	2559	2863	2392	1882	2140	2211	2181	1837	1086	2149	2080	2072	1627
Springfield, Ill.	969	600	754	1138	696	193	301	510	365	795	863	459	906	192	306
Springfield, Mo.	1245	725	1077	1411	949	522	564	761	635	472	817	733	674	461	174
Syracuse, N. Y.	139	1014	327	309	153	685	595	344	490	1558	1704	405	1700	641	1137
Tampa, Fla.	1370	482	1010	1396	1378	1194	954	1160	1071	1101	1901	1216	1057	1036	1292
Toledo, Ohio.	572	678	454	741	296	239	198	110	128	1149	1254	57	1251	220	710
Toronto, Ont.	400	1014	468	570	100	542	500	288	426	1453	1559	238	1545	510	1004
Tulsa, Okla.	1444	830	1276	1610	1128	720	765	960	834	278	701	932	521	660	249
Vancouver, B. C.	3121	2890	2971	3300	2830	2313	2594	2642	2612	2294	1498	2561	2537	2484	2075
Washington, D. C.	369	648	38	437	361	685	492	351	395	1402	1614	511	1482	568	1059
Wichita, Kans.	1496	1014	1348	1662	1200	741	815	1012	868	385	515	964	628	712	198
Wilmington, N. C.	757	441	398	796	766	961	682	739	645	1255	1876	836	1305	792	1234
Winnipeg, Man.	1643	1584	1620	1808	1421	877	1178	1226	1196	1375	1105	1203	1618	1067	908

TO \ FROM	Los Angeles, Cal.	Louisville, Ky.	Memphis, Tenn.	Miami, Fla.	Minneapolis-St. Paul	New Orleans, La.	New York, N. Y.	Omaha, Neb.	Philadelphia, Pa.	Richmond, Va.	St. Louis, Mo.	Salt Lake City, Utah	San Francisco, Cal.	Seattle, Wash.	Washington, D.C.
Miami, Fla.	2817	1121	1030	....	1803	900	1350	1728	1247	1015	1259	2600	3219	3454	1123
Milwaukee, Wis.	2199	394	638	1477	337	1030	935	498	848	877	367	1465	2223	2055	773
Minneapolis-St. Paul	2018	719	863	1803	....	1263	1261	364	1172	1203	562	1283	2042	1642	1108
Mobile, Ala.	2042	634	373	775	1304	152	1240	1062	1148	926	642	1877	2444	2701	1013
Montgomery, Ala.	2102	491	345	730	1176	340	1052	1047	960	738	638	1961	2504	2775	825
Montreal, Que.	3022	959	1309	1742	1150	1602	392	1348	495	724	1106	2303	3060	2747	619
Nashville, Tenn.	2091	183	220	929	868	568	930	806	840	628	330	1734	2424	2516	703
New Orleans, La.	1951	751	403	900	1263	....	1365	1080	1261	1050	701	1808	2300	2658	1138
New York, N. Y.	2913	790	1155	1350	1261	1365	....	1300	92	332	962	2303	3062	2975	225
Oklahoma City, Okla.	1386	797	485	1525	852	679	1517	488	1437	1354	530	1106	1719	1920	1368
Omaha, Neb.	1701	704	680	1728	364	1080	1300	....	1243	1222	469	966	1725	1735	1155
Philadelphia, Pa.	2823	700	1059	1247	1172	1261	92	1225	....	240	885	2209	2968	2875	135
Phoenix, Ariz.	403	1793	1481	2414	1743	1548	2500	1349	2501	2350	1526	720	828	1535	2364
Pittsburgh, Pa.	2547	395	798	1258	874	1125	386	950	305	352	596	1916	2675	2611	230
Portland, Me.	3179	1080	1468	1696	1480	1714	313	1515	406	645	1263	2470	3233	3016	540
Portland, Ore.	1004	2489	2442	3482	1585	2634	3111	1778	3002	3000	2222	826	674	176	2931
Providence, R. I.	3092	969	1334	1562	1426	1544	183	1516	271	511	1242	2428	3183	3154	404
Quebec, Que.	3195	1132	1482	1915	1323	1775	565	1521	665	897	1295	2470	3233	2920	792
Raleigh, N. C.	2659	598	793	848	1281	926	491	1334	399	159	865	2310	2997	3044	264
Rapid City, S. D.	1421	1272	1251	2293	597	1630	1772	549	1679	1789	1005	686	1445	1197	1635
Richmond, Va.	2740	577	869	1015	1203	1050	332	1222	240	....	844	2198	2957	2940	105
Sacramento, Cal.	386	2334	2174	3189	1953	2322	2976	1636	2882	2868	2067	670	89	794	2789
St. Joseph, Mo.	1772	578	544	1586	436	922	1246	158	1156	1122	311	1072	1831	1866	1053
St. Louis, Mo.	1916	267	301	1259	562	701	962	469	885	844	....	1397	2156	2251	806
Salt Lake City, Utah	735	1664	1616	2600	1283	1808	2303	966	2191	2209	1397	....	759	889	2119
San Antonio, Tex.	1379	1142	739	1525	1259	581	1894	953	1798	1580	966	1426	1804	2305	1667
San Diego, Cal.	124	2158	1846	2744	2068	1878	2888	1714	2798	2715	1891	785	556		2729
San Francisco, Cal.	408	2423	2204	3219	2042	2300	3062	1725	2968	2957	2156	759	....	850	2878
Santa Fe, N. M.	896	1339	1027	2016	1307	1149	2069	905	1992	1896	1072	625	1229	1514	1941
Sault Ste. Marie	2555	634	964	1753	537	1367	937	901	941	988	727	1820	2579	2134	887
Scranton, Pa.	2860	718	1112	1366	1162	1415	125	1229	122	341	873	2163	2922	2919	257
Seattle, Wash.	1190	2446	2430	3454	1642	2658	2975	1735	2875	2940	2251	889	850	....	2845
Shreveport, La.	1630	753	350	1187	1029	320	1505	777	1409	1191	572	1465	2032	2279	1241
Sioux City, Ia.	1714	829	808	1830	336	1186	1336	106	1247	1326	562	996	1755	1640	1203
Sioux Falls, S. D.	1752	917	896	1918	248	1274	1414	194	1325	1414	650	1053	1812	1555	1261
Spokane, Wash.	1261	2151	2135	3159	1347	2344	2708	1440	2619	2650	1884	756	939	295	2555
Springfield, Ill.	2034	280	404	1296	502	804	944	446	926	820	101	1374	2133	2238	751
Springfield, Mo.	1696	487	316	1391	602	694	1217	386	1127	1132	220	1314	2029	2096	1058
Syracuse, N. Y.	2798	703	1109	1489	1106	1349	301	1147	262	471	882	2102	2893	2840	366
Tampa, Fla.	2544	922	802	272	1633	672	1229	1504	1096	863	1068	2383	2946	3232	971
Toledo, Ohio	2373	314	660	1359	637	1060	610	704	529	590	506	1659	2422	2414	454
Toronto, Ont.	2667	608	954	1630	957	1354	527	1004	498	612	751	1957	2705	2587	507
Tulsa, Okla.	1497	686	427	1467	713	713	1416	401	1326	1331	419	1189	1830	2003	1257
Vancouver, B. C.	1364	2563	2447	3607	1759	2840	3144	1852	3031	3062	2296	1032	993	143	2967
Washington, D. C.	2754	602	928	1123	1108	1138	225	1155	135	105	806	2119	2878	2845	....
Wichita, Kans.	1509	738	611	1659	678	853	1448	314	1358	1315	471	1003	1762	1817	1309
Wilmington, N. C.	2698	708	855	778	1376	927	580	1391	477	254	975	2379	3085	3156	359
Winnipeg, Man.	2120	1223	1343	2265	457	1746	1773	696	1670	1665	1042	1385	2144	1473	1571

Appendix IV
Monthly Expense "Spread Sheets"

These "spread sheets" are intended to provide you with the means of doing some easy bookkeeping as the year goes on, thereby reducing the amount of work necessary to file your return at year's end. Those items with asterisks (†astericesê to you, Mr. Buckley) must be backed up by receipted evidence no matter how small.

The categorization is not arbitrary on my part. For example, hotel or airport tips while you are travelling may be used to account for reported per diem but tips to dressers in your tax home may not.

Feel free to adapt the "spread sheets" to suit your needs, but keep in mind all the substantiation rules. (See pages 15, 44 *et seq.*)

Year ___ Month ___ Day	Out of Town Meals	Out of Town Lodging*	Out of Town Laundry & Cleaning	Out of Town Local Transport	Rental Car & Gas*	Business Mileage on Personal Car	Tolls and Parking*	Traveling Tips (Hotel, Air Porter)	Air, Rail for Business*
1									
2									
3									
4									
5									
6									
7									
8									
9									
10									
11									
12									
13									
14									
15									
16									
17									
18									
19									
20									
21									
22									
23									
24									
25									
26									
27									
28									
29									
30									
31									
Monthly TOTALS									

Local Transp. for Interviews, Auditions	Dresser, Doorman Tips	Trade Papers	Coin Phone for Business	Business Meals (Entertainment) (over $25*)	Other Deductible Local Transp.			Name of Location of out-of-town job	
									1
									2
									3
									4
									5
									6
									7
									8
									9
									10
									11
									12
									13
									14
									15
									16
									17
									18
									19
									20
									21
									22
									23
									24
									25
									26
									27
									28
									29
									30
									31

Year ___ Month ___ Day	Out of Town Meals	Out of Town Lodging*	Out of Town Laundry & Cleaning	Out of Town Local Transport	Rental Car & Gas*	Business Mileage on Personal Car	Tolls and Parking*	Traveling Tips (Hotel, Air Porter)	Air, Rail for Business*
1									
2									
3									
4									
5									
6									
7									
8									
9									
10									
11									
12									
13									
14									
15									
16									
17									
18									
19									
20									
21									
22									
23									
24									
25									
26									
27									
28									
29									
30									
31									
Monthly TOTALS									

Local Transp. for Interviews, Auditions	Dresser, Doorman Tips	Trade Papers	Coin Phone for Business	Business Meals (Entertainment) (over $25*)	Other Deductible Local Transp.			Name of Location of out-ot-town job	
									1
									2
									3
									4
									5
									6
									7
									8
									9
									10
									11
									12
									13
									14
									15
									16
									17
									18
									19
									20
									21
									22
									23
									24
									25
									26
									27
									28
									29
									30
									31

113

Year ___ Month ___ Day	Out of Town Meals	Out of Town Lodging*	Out of Town Laundry & Cleaning	Out of Town Local Transport	Rental Car & Gas*	Business Mileage on Personal Car	Tolls and Parking*	Traveling Tips (Hotel, Air Porter)	Air, Rail for Business*
1									
2									
3									
4									
5									
6									
7									
8									
9									
10									
11									
12									
13									
14									
15									
16									
17									
18									
19									
20									
21									
22									
23									
24									
25									
26									
27									
28									
29									
30									
31									
Monthly TOTALS									

Local Transp. for Interviews, Auditions	Dresser, Doorman Tips	Trade Papers	Coin Phone for Business	Business Meals (Entertainment) (over $25*)	Other Deductible Local Transp.			Name of Location of out-ot-town job	
									1
									2
									3
									4
									5
									6
									7
									8
									9
									10
									11
									12
									13
									14
									15
									16
									17
									18
									19
									20
									21
									22
									23
									24
									25
									26
									27
									28
									29
									30
									31

Year ___ Month ___ Day	Out of Town Meals	Out of Town Lodging*	Out of Town Laundry & Cleaning	Out of Town Local Transport	Rental Car & Gas*	Business Mileage on Personal Car	Tolls and Parking*	Traveling Tips (Hotel, Air Porter)	Air, Rail for Business*
1									
2									
3									
4									
5									
6									
7									
8									
9									
10									
11									
12									
13									
14									
15									
16									
17									
18									
19									
20									
21									
22									
23									
24									
25									
26									
27									
28									
29									
30									
31									
Monthly TOTALS									

Local Transp. for Interviews, Auditions	Dresser, Doorman Tips	Trade Papers	Coin Phone for Business	Business Meals (Entertainment) (over $25*)	Other Deductible Local Transp.			Name of Location of out-ot-town job	
									1
									2
									3
									4
									5
									6
									7
									8
									9
									10
									11
									12
									13
									14
									15
									16
									17
									18
									19
									20
									21
									22
									23
									24
									25
									26
									27
									28
									29
									30
									31

Year ___ Month ___ Day	Out of Town Meals	Out of Town Lodging*	Out of Town Laundry & Cleaning	Out of Town Local Transport	Rental Car & Gas*	Business Mileage on Personal Car	Tolls and Parking*	Traveling Tips (Hotel, Air Porter)	Air, Rail for Business*
1									
2									
3									
4									
5									
6									
7									
8									
9									
10									
11									
12									
13									
14									
15									
16									
17									
18									
19									
20									
21									
22									
23									
24									
25									
26									
27									
28									
29									
30									
31									
Monthly TOTALS									

Local Transp. for Interviews, Auditions	Dresser, Doorman Tips	Trade Papers	Coin Phone for Business	Business Meals (Entertainment) (over $25*)	Other Deductible Local Transp.			Name of Location of out-of-town job	
									1
									2
									3
									4
									5
									6
									7
									8
									9
									10
									11
									12
									13
									14
									15
									16
									17
									18
									19
									20
									21
									22
									23
									24
									25
									26
									27
									28
									29
									30
									31

Year ___ Month ___ Day	Out of Town Meals	Out of Town Lodging*	Out of Town Laundry & Cleaning	Out of Town Local Transport	Rental Car & Gas*	Business Mileage on Personal Car	Tolls and Parking*	Traveling Tips (Hotel, Air Porter)	Air, Rail for Business*
1									
2									
3									
4									
5									
6									
7									
8									
9									
10									
11									
12									
13									
14									
15									
16									
17									
18									
19									
20									
21									
22									
23									
24									
25									
26									
27									
28									
29									
30									
31									
Monthly TOTALS									

Local Transp. for Interviews, Auditions	Dresser, Doorman Tips	Trade Papers	Coin Phone for Business	Business Meals (Entertainment) (over $25*)	Other Deductible Local Transp.			Name of Location of out-ot-town job	
									1
									2
									3
									4
									5
									6
									7
									8
									9
									10
									11
									12
									13
									14
									15
									16
									17
									18
									19
									20
									21
									22
									23
									24
									25
									26
									27
									28
									29
									30
									31

Year ___ Month ___ Day	Out of Town Meals	Out of Town Lodging*	Out of Town Laundry & Cleaning	Out of Town Local Transport	Rental Car & Gas*	Business Mileage on Personal Car	Tolls and Parking*	Traveling Tips (Hotel, Air Porter)	Air, Rail for Business*
1									
2									
3									
4									
5									
6									
7									
8									
9									
10									
11									
12									
13									
14									
15									
16									
17									
18									
19									
20									
21									
22									
23									
24									
25									
26									
27									
28									
29									
30									
31									
Monthly TOTALS									

Local Transp. for Interviews, Auditions	Dresser, Doorman Tips	Trade Papers	Coin Phone for Business	Business Meals (Entertainment) (over $25*)	Other Deductible Local Transp.			Name of Location of out-of-town job	
									1
									2
									3
									4
									5
									6
									7
									8
									9
									10
									11
									12
									13
									14
									15
									16
									17
									18
									19
									20
									21
									22
									23
									24
									25
									26
									27
									28
									29
									30
									31

Year ___ Month ___ Day	Out of Town Meals	Out of Town Lodging*	Out of Town Laundry & Cleaning	Out of Town Local Transport	Rental Car & Gas*	Business Mileage on Personal Car	Tolls and Parking*	Traveling Tips (Hotel, Air Porter)	Air, Rail for Business*
1									
2									
3									
4									
5									
6									
7									
8									
9									
10									
11									
12									
13									
14									
15									
16									
17									
18									
19									
20									
21									
22									
23									
24									
25									
26									
27									
28									
29									
30									
31									
Monthly TOTALS									

Local Transp. for Interviews, Auditions	Dresser, Doorman Tips	Trade Papers	Coin Phone for Business	Business Meals (Entertainment) (over $25*)	Other Deductible Local Transp.			Name of Location of out-of-town job	
									1
									2
									3
									4
									5
									6
									7
									8
									9
									10
									11
									12
									13
									14
									15
									16
									17
									18
									19
									20
									21
									22
									23
									24
									25
									26
									27
									28
									29
									30
									31

Year ___ Month ___ Day	Out of Town Meals	Out of Town Lodging*	Out of Town Laundry & Cleaning	Out of Town Local Transport	Rental Car & Gas*	Business Mileage on Personal Car	Tolls and Parking*	Traveling Tips (Hotel, Air Porter)	Air, Rail for Business*
1									
2									
3									
4									
5									
6									
7									
8									
9									
10									
11									
12									
13									
14									
15									
16									
17									
18									
19									
20									
21									
22									
23									
24									
25									
26									
27									
28									
29									
30									
31									
Monthly TOTALS									

Local Transp. for Interviews, Auditions	Dresser, Doorman Tips	Trade Papers	Coin Phone for Business	Business Meals (Entertainment) (over $25*)	Other Deductible Local Transp.			Name of Location of out-ot-town job	
									1
									2
									3
									4
									5
									6
									7
									8
									9
									10
									11
									12
									13
									14
									15
									16
									17
									18
									19
									20
									21
									22
									23
									24
									25
									26
									27
									28
									29
									30
									31

Year ───── Month ───── Day	Out of Town Meals	Out of Town Lodging*	Out of Town Laundry & Cleaning	Out of Town Local Transport	Rental Car & Gas*	Business Mileage on Personal Car	Tolls and Parking*	Traveling Tips (Hotel, Air Porter)	Air, Rail for Business*
1									
2									
3									
4									
5									
6									
7									
8									
9									
10									
11									
12									
13									
14									
15									
16									
17									
18									
19									
20									
21									
22									
23									
24									
25									
26									
27									
28									
29									
30									
31									
Monthly TOTALS									

Local Transp. for Interviews, Auditions	Dresser, Doorman Tips	Trade Papers	Coin Phone for Business	Business Meals (Entertainment) (over $25")	Other Deductible Local Transp.			Name of Location of out-ot-town job	
									1
									2
									3
									4
									5
									6
									7
									8
									9
									10
									11
									12
									13
									14
									15
									16
									17
									18
									19
									20
									21
									22
									23
									24
									25
									26
									27
									28
									29
									30
									31

Year ___ Month ___ Day	Out of Town Meals	Out of Town Lodging*	Out of Town Laundry & Cleaning	Out of Town Local Transport	Rental Car & Gas*	Business Mileage on Personal Car	Tolls and Parking*	Traveling Tips (Hotel, Air Porter)	Air, Rail for Business*
1									
2									
3									
4									
5									
6									
7									
8									
9									
10									
11									
12									
13									
14									
15									
16									
17									
18									
19									
20									
21									
22									
23									
24									
25									
26									
27									
28									
29									
30									
31									
Monthly TOTALS									

Local Transp. for Interviews, Auditions	Dresser, Doorman Tips	Trade Papers	Coin Phone for Business	Business Meals (Entertainment) (over $25*)	Other Deductible Local Transp.			Name of Location of out-ot-town job	
									1
									2
									3
									4
									5
									6
									7
									8
									9
									10
									11
									12
									13
									14
									15
									16
									17
									18
									19
									20
									21
									22
									23
									24
									25
									26
									27
									28
									29
									30
									31

Year ___ Month ___ Day	Out of Town Meals	Out of Town Lodging*	Out of Town Laundry & Cleaning	Out of Town Local Transport	Rental Car & Gas*	Business Mileage on Personal Car	Tolls and Parking*	Traveling Tips (Hotel, Air Porter)	Air, Rail for Business*
1									
2									
3									
4									
5									
6									
7									
8									
9									
10									
11									
12									
13									
14									
15									
16									
17									
18									
19									
20									
21									
22									
23									
24									
25									
26									
27									
28									
29									
30									
31									
Monthly TOTALS									

Local Transp. for Interviews, Auditions	Dresser, Doorman Tips	Trade Papers	Coin Phone for Business	Business Meals (Entertainment) (over $25*)	Other Deductible Local Transp.			Name of Location of out-of-town job	
									1
									2
									3
									4
									5
									6
									7
									8
									9
									10
									11
									12
									13
									14
									15
									16
									17
									18
									19
									20
									21
									22
									23
									24
									25
									26
									27
									28
									29
									30
									31

Appendix V
Record of Exemptions Claimed

Job	Date W-4 Submitted	# of Exemptions	Amended Y or N?

Job	Date W-4 Submitted	# of Exemptions	Amended Y or N?

Job	Date W-4 Submitted	# of Exemptions	Amended Y or N?

Job	Date W-4 Submitted	# of Exemptions	Amended Y or N?

ABOUT THE AUTHOR

BRENDAN HANLON studied theatre at Emerson College and Smith College. There followed a varied career in show business: clowning, five seasons in regional theatre, television, and clubs. He composed the song "Ketchup, Indiana (Blues)," which paid the rent for eight months. His last Off-Broadway show convinced him to seek his fortune and the bubble reputation as an income tax preparer. In addition to this tax book, Mr. Hanlon has written articles for *Theatre Crafts* and *Equity News* and is a frequent speaker at theatre conferences and performing arts colleges. He now lives with his wife and daughter in Massachusetts. In addition to the occasional acting job, he has been producing the Fine Performance Series at The First Parish Church, Universalist Unitarian in Duxbury. This series brings Metropolitan Opera stars, all-star jazz ensembles, and classic and baroque music to the South Shore of the Massachusetts coast.